NOTTINGHAM

NOTTINGHAM

*The Buried Past of a Historic
City Revealed*

Scott Lomax

First published in Great Britain in 2013 by
PEN & SWORD ARCHAEOLOGY
an imprint of
Pen and Sword Books Ltd
47 Church Street
Barnsley
South Yorkshire S70 2AS

ISBN 978 1 78159 389 9

A CIP record for this book is available from the British Library

Printed and bound in England
by CPI Group (UK) Ltd, Croydon, CR0 4YY

Typeset in Times New Roman by
CHIC GRAPHICS

Pen & Sword Books Ltd incorporates the imprints of
Pen & Sword Archaeology, Atlas, Aviation, Battleground, Discovery,
Family History, History, Maritime, Military, Naval, Politics, Railways,
Select, Social History, Transport, True Crime, and Claymore Press,
Frontline Books, Leo Cooper, Praetorian Press, Remember When,
Seaforth Publishing and Wharncliffe.

For a complete list of Pen and Sword titles please contact
Pen and Sword Books Limited
47 Church Street, Barnsley, South Yorkshire, S70 2AS, England
E-mail: enquiries@pen-and-sword.co.uk
Website: www.pen-and-sword.co.uk

Contents

A statue of the legendary outlaw Robin Hood, which stands on Castle Road. (The Author)

There's More to Nottingham Than Robin Hood

The tales of Robin Hood epitomise the popular perception of what Nottingham and its folk were like in medieval times. Beyond the ballads and other texts, however, there has been real evidence uncovered for Nottingham's past which in many ways is more interesting than what is to many a work of fiction. Certainly there is far more to Nottingham than Robin Hood and it is hoped this book will provide the reader with an outline of what the practice of archaeology has contributed to our understanding of the development of Nottingham over the course of thousands of years. Take for example the knowledge from historic texts that the Danish army had winter quarters in Nottingham in 868 and was later occupied by the Norse.[1] During the Victorian period the skeletons of two men, buried with weapons, were found to date to the ninth century[2] and archaeological work of the twentieth century has shown the extent of the Viking town. Yet Nottingham's connections with the Vikings are little known of. The same is true of many aspects of Nottingham's past, as you will discover.

In 1813 a local historian wrote that 'perhaps there is no other town in the kingdom whose origin is hid in greater obscurity than Nottingham'.[3] This is as true today as it was two hundred years ago and this book aims to rectify that situation.

I will concentrate on that area known to archaeologists as the historic core; the area of the medieval town of Nottingham. Readers may wonder why I refer to the area discussed as being a town rather than a city. This is because Nottingham only became a city during the Victorian period and up until reasonably modern times the outlying parts of the city were individual places in their own rights. Certainly until the late-medieval period the historic core stood alone, largely enclosed within defences, with the town's authorities having power only over the land and people contained within.

Despite the richness of historical sources relating to Nottingham's past it is the largely recent results of archaeological work which are discussed here. Often existing documentation is vague. It may refer to buildings, features and even places but not describe their nature or exact location.

Documentation and archaeological work must nonetheless go hand in hand. Archaeology supplements, and is supplemented by, documentation. Documentation can help date archaeological deposits when they can be identified in historic texts and archaeology can help confirm what is said in documentation or shown on historic plans. However, sometimes archaeology contradicts what is referred to in the texts, which may have been based upon misinformation or bias or just be simply incorrect, and often archaeology cannot explain what was written in the past. Sometimes archaeology reveals something about the past that was not previously known from any historic source, and that is a huge part of the fun of the discipline. Archaeological excavations in Nottingham have provided details of the buildings in which people lived, the agricultural activities and industries they carried out, the caves they constructed, the defences within which their occupation was constrained until the seventeenth century and the places where they worshipped. All of these aspects are covered in this book.

The historic core of Nottingham has undergone large scale redevelopment over a number of centuries. In the days before archaeological investigation this led to important remains being destroyed (especially by deep cellars and foundations for buildings and also the stripping down to the natural bedrock before new construction work takes place). However, more recent redevelopment, especially during the second half of the twentieth century, provided opportunities to investigate large amounts of the historic core of Nottingham.

The development of Maid Marian Way and creation of a bus station at Park Row/Cumberland Place, construction of the Broadmarsh Shopping Centre and the Ice Centre, redevelopment on the site of the former General Hospital and creation of buildings across the city centre has transformed the appearance of the city and in striving towards modernity the city has destroyed many of its links to the past.

Nonetheless the entirety of the city centre, with the castle at the west and the Ice Centre at the east, extending towards the River Trent with a small corridor along London Road has been designated an Archaeological Constraint Area in the City Council's Local Development Framework in recognition of the potential for archaeological remains to survive, although how much actually still survives is uncertain.

This book will only describe a small portion of the archaeological work undertaken in the historic core. There have been more than 500 recorded investigations by archaeologists or individuals who have found something that contributes to our knowledge of Nottingham's past. These investigations have been in the form of excavations, watching briefs (where groundworks such as the digging of foundations or the laying of water pipes or other utilities have been observed by an archaeologist), geophysical or other non-invasive surveys, for example probing for subterranean features, borehole sampling or aerial photography.

Between 2008 and 2010 I established, for Nottingham City Council, the Nottingham Urban Archaeological Database, a database linked to a Geographical Information System which provides a fully mapped and searchable record of archaeology within the historic core.[4] I also worked as a researcher on the Nottingham Caves Survey Project with Trent & Peak Archaeology, researching Nottingham's extensive man-made cave systems. During this work I uncovered information that had been lost in archives, sometimes for decades, and it is the knowledge I have acquired during this work, and additional extensive research, which has enabled me to present the very first popular guide to Nottingham's archaeology.

Since the text of this book was written a project which I am involved in called 'The Origins of Nottingham' has commenced to look at six important excavations in the medieval town.[5] The project is managed by Trent & Peak Archaeology, in partnership with Nottingham City Council, and is funded by English Heritage. If the project continues to receive funding to allow detailed research to be undertaken then it will really help provide in-depth knowledge of various aspects of archaeology in Nottingham. Such analysis is crucial but it is also essential to provide a general overview of Nottingham's archaeology for a general audience. Those wanting more in depth knowledge should hope that The Origins of Nottingham goes the full way. This book is intended, however, to be a starting point for those wanting to explore Nottingham's past, be they local people, school or university students, or archaeologists.

Whilst this book has used the Nottingham Urban Archaeological Database as one of its many sources, additional extensive research of primary sources has been undertaken specifically for this book. The Urban Archaeological Database contains a lot of detailed information which it is not necessary to include in this general overview of the city's past. In fact only a small proportion of the sites included in the Urban Archaeological Database will be referred to in this book.

Other sources used in the writing of this book include the county archaeology and local history journal *Transactions of the Thoroton Society of Nottinghamshire*, several antiquarian books referred to in the text where appropriate, archaeological reports which are in the public domain via the Nottingham City Council website and the Archaeological Data Service website,[6] English Heritage's National Monuments Record and various books available at Nottingham Central Library Local Studies department.

My thanks go to Gordon Young, Nottingham's City Archaeologist for our frequent discussions about archaeology over the years and also to Nick Tomlinson of Picture the Past for assisting me with obtaining some of the images to use in this book. I would also like to thank Eloise Hansen of Pen and Sword Archaeology and all the staff at Pen and Sword Books.

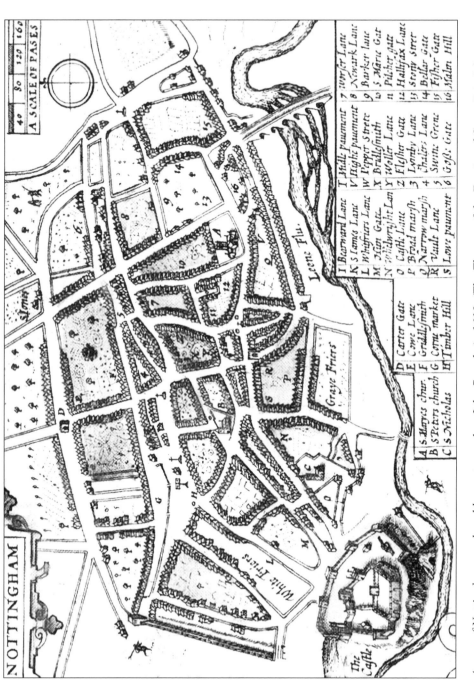

A map of Nottingham produced by cartographer John Speede in 1610. (The Theatre of the Empire of Great Britain)

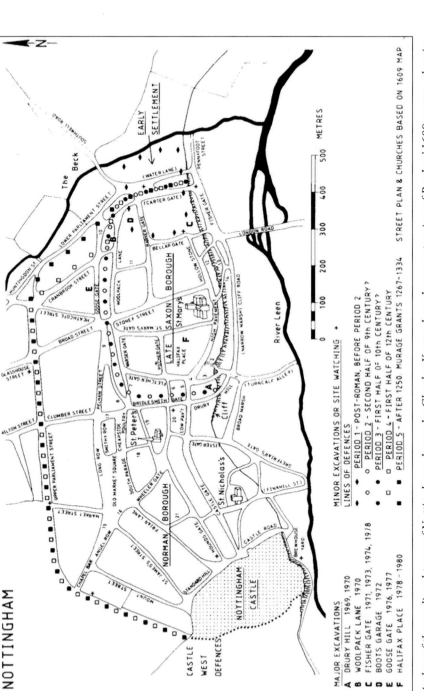

A plan of the medieval town of Nottingham, drawn by Charles Young, based upon a tracing of Bankes' 1609 survey, showing the earliest known street patterns. It shows the projected lines of the defences of the pre-Conquest borough and post-Conquest, medieval, town. The locations of the 'Big Six' excavations are also indicated. (Nottingham City Museums and Galleries)

Glossary

Archaeological Constraint Area – An area determined by Nottingham City Council's Local Plan and to be incorporated into the new Local Development Framework, which identifies parts of the city which may have important archaeological remains that need to be considered as part of the planning process.

Danelaw – In 877 King Alfred made a truce with Guthrum, leader of the invading Danes, which resulted in England being divided into the Danelaw and the Anglo-Saxon southern kingdom.

Desk Based Assessment – A written assessment which provides the results of research of historic sources and previous archaeological work, in order to establish the likelihood of archaeological remains surviving on the site of a proposed development. The desk based assessment attempts to assess the impact of a development upon buried archaeological remains and any standing buildings of historic significance. The desk based assessment will provide recommendations as to what, if any, further archaeological work should take place to mitigate potential impacts.

English Borough – Following the Norman Conquest the former Saxon settlement became the English Borough, which, over time, expanded northwards and westwards towards the Market Square.[7]

Evaluation – A small excavation (usually in the form of one or more machine dug trenches) to evaluate how much archaeology survives on the site. If the evaluation establishes that there is sufficient archaeology present then a larger scale excavation may take place.

Excavation – The exposure, processing and recording of archaeological remains on a larger scale than an evaluation.

Findspot - Residual solitary artefacts or assemblages of artefacts.

Five Boroughs – Derby, Leicester, Lincoln, Nottingham and Stamford were five fortified boroughs under Danish rule, or Danelaw, between 877 and 918.[8]

French Borough – The French Borough comprised of the western most part of the medieval town of Nottingham, including the Castle.[9]

Historic Core – In the case of Nottingham the historic core is the area of the medieval town, with Castle Boulevard and Canal Street at the southern limit and Parliament Street forming the remainder of its perimeter, with a small corridor extending along London Road towards the Trent Bridge.

Murage Grants – Between 1267 and 1337 grants known as murage grants were levied to raise funds to build the town wall.[10]

National Planning Policy Framework – Legislation introduced in March 2012 by the Department for the Communities and Local Government. The relevant section of the Framework is headed 'Conserving and enhancing the historic environment' and it sets out to achieve this aim by recognising that the historic environment makes a positive contribution to society, the economy, culture and the environment. The impact of a proposed development on heritage assets must be considered when determining whether a planning application should be approved.[11]

Nottingham Castle Sandstone - The natural bedrock of the historic core of Nottingham. It has previously been known as Bunter Sandstone. Nottingham's man-made caves are cut into this soft, porous and relatively fine-grained sandstone, containing pebbles, which was laid down during the Triassic period approximately 250 million years ago.[12]

Planning Policy Guidance Note 16 – In November 1990 the Government issued PPG 16, 'Archaeology and Planning' which expressed a desire to preserve ancient monuments. Local authorities were advised that damage to archaeological sites could be a justifiable reason to refuse planning permission. It also allowed local authorities to request that a Desk Based Assessment be produced and, if necessary, archaeological fieldwork be undertaken in advance of development to record any archaeological remains, at the expense of the developer. PPG16 was adopted by Nottingham City Council in 1992.

Pre-Conquest Borough – The late-Saxon settlement of Nottingham which is coterminous with the present day Lace Market, which was bounded by a defensive ditch.[13]

Post-Conquest Borough – The medieval town of Nottingham following the Norman Conquest of 1066 and the building of Nottingham's first castle in 1068.

Residual – Artefacts which predate the layers in which they are found.

Robber Trench – A robber trench is a hole in the ground dug in historic times to take away materials, usually stone, to re-use them. For example, if a stone wall was known to exist beneath the ground, made of good quality stone, and a new stone wall needed to be built it would be sensible to dig up the old wall and reuse the stone.

Stratigraphy – Layers in the ground, both natural and man-made, and features cutting into those layers which show how a site has developed over time. Artefacts in each layer can help date that development. Unfortunately in parts of Nottingham, unlike most cities, there is a lack of stratigraphy. This is because in most parts of the area of the medieval town deposits were stripped prior to redevelopment taking place. This means that often only features cut into the natural sandstone bedrock survive. Deeper stratigraphy survives to the south, where the River Leen once flowed.

Watching Brief – When development of a site commences an archaeologist may monitor the site and undertake recording and any necessary excavation of features revealed. This is known as a watching brief.

Timeline

Neolithic (c. 4000 – 2500 BC)

Evidence for Neolithic occupation and activity is scant. A polished stone hammer found close to the River Trent may have dated to the Neolithic or early Bronze Age.[14]

A Neolithic or early Bronze Age sandstone axe head was found on the site of the Moot Hall public house, which once stood on Friar Lane.[15] Residual Neolithic flint implements have also occasionally been found in the backfill of caves.

Bronze Age (c. 2500 – 800 BC)

There is also little evidence for Bronze Age occupation and activity. In addition to the polished stone hammer and sandstone axe head referred to above, which may date to the Bronze Age, a looped and socketed spearhead was 'fished-up' from the River Trent,[16] a Bronze Age sword was dredged from the riverbed at West Bridgford, a Middle Bronze Age palstave and a Late Bronze Age socketed axe were found at Chapel Bar,[17] a hoard of Bronze Age weapons was found during the building of the Theatre Royal,[18] and a hoard of damaged Bronze Age implements were found at Great Freeman Street.[19] A flint arrowhead dating to this period was found in Sneinton.[20]

Iron Age (800 BC – 43 AD)

Some occupation and activity was taking place at this time. Tentative evidence of Iron Age farmsteads have been found at Fisher Gate and Halifax Place.[21] There may also have been occupation of land immediately north of Nottingham Castle.[22]

Roman (43 – 410 AD)

Evidence of Roman occupation or activity is limited to a small number of residual sherds of pottery found in the backfill of caves and in numerous features excavated within the area of the medieval town.

Early-Saxon (410 – 650)
No artefacts dating to this period have been found within the area of the medieval town. No features or deposits have therefore been dated to the early Saxon period.

Middle Saxon (c. 650 – 850)
At least two parts of the Lace Market were occupied during this period; at Halifax Place to the west and land between Fisher Gate and Barker Gate to the east (on the site of the Ice Stadium).[23]

Late-Saxon (c. 850 – 1066)
868-869 - Vikings wintered in Nottingham. The Anglo-Saxon Chronicle records:

> 'A.D. 868. This year the same army went into Mercia to Nottingham, and there fixed their winter-quarters ; and Burhred king of the Mercians, with his council, besought Ethered, king of the West-Saxons, and Alfred, his brother, that they would assist them in fighting against the army. And they went with the West-Saxon army into Mercia as far as Nottingham, and there meeting the army on the works, they beset them with-in. But there was no heavy fight; for the Mercians made peace with the army.'[24]

873 - A Scandinavian settlement was recorded at Nottingham.[25]

877–918 - Nottingham was one of the five Boroughs of the Danelaw.[26]

918 - By this year, the pre-Conquest borough was surrounded by a rampart and ditch and protected to the south by a natural cliff. In this year Edward the Elder is recorded as having recaptured the town from the Danes and strengthened its defences.[27]

920 - Edward the Elder constructed another fortification on the south side of the river. This is believed to be West Bridgford but could be Wilford.[28]

928 - Nottingham was given permission to found a mint. The town had two moneyers.[29]

939 - Norwegian troops, under the leadership of Olaf Guthfrithson, conquered the towns of the East Midlands, including Nottingham, destroying the systems of the Five Boroughs.[30]

942 - King Edmund recaptured the town from the Norse.[31]

Medieval (1066 – 1540)
1068 - A timber castle was built on the Castle Rock.[32]

1086 - By this year the pre-Conquest ditch had been filled in and twenty-three houses have been built on where the ditch once existed. The Domesday Survey completed in 1086 recorded that Nottingham had forty-eight merchant's houses, two moneyers and a church.[33]

1171 - The earth and timber fortifications of the castle began to be replaced by stone.[34]

1230 - By this year the Franciscans/Grey Friars had been founded in the south-west corner of Broad Marsh.[35]

1267 - The first murage grant was levied towards the cost of building the medieval town wall.[36]

1272 - By this year the Carmelite/White Friars friary was established between St James's Street and Friar Lane.[37]

c. 1350 - Much of the area around St Mary's Church was abandoned.[38]

1395 - The first reference was made to the medieval town wall being robbed.[39]

1433–1434 - A Royal Charter labelled Nottingham as an impoverished town.[40]

1535/36 - A Royal Order from Henry VIII states that many houses in Nottingham were in 'great ruin and decay' and that there were 'pyttes, cellars and vaults, lying open and uncovered, very perillous for people to go by in the Nyghte withoute Jeopardy of Lyf.'[41]

Post medieval (1540 – 1901)
1540 - With the Dissolution of the Monasteries, Nottingham's two friaries and St John's Hospital ceased to have a religious role.[42]

1603 - By this year the medieval castle was no longer occupied, had fallen into disrepair and was partly pulled down.[43]

1610 - By this year the town had begun to gradually expand beyond the medieval defences. Speede's map of 1610 shows two rows of dwellings north of the line of the town wall. Pottery production has long taken place beyond the town wall.[44]

1642 - King Charles I raised the Royal Standard at Standard Hill, commencing the English Civil War.[45]

1642–46 - The Parliamentarians held the town.[46]

1651 - No longer required, the castle was destroyed with gunpowder much to the dismay of Oliver Cromwell.[47]

1674 - The Duke of Newcastle cleared away the medieval structure of the castle except for parts of the wall and the gatehouse.[48]

1679 - The Ducal Palace was built on the site of the medieval castle, under the instruction of the Duke of Newcastle who never lived to see its completion. His successor moved into the Ducal Palace and made alterations.[49]

1714 - The French and English Boroughs merged to form a single town.[50]

Antiquarians and Amateur Archaeology

Nottingham has a long tradition of dedicated antiquarians and amateur archaeologists whose work and observations have helped shape our understanding of Nottingham's past and raised questions about many aspects of the historic core which professional archaeology has tried to resolve. Here I will outline some of the main characters and organizations, and some of their contributions which will be further detailed in later chapters.

There are many historic accounts of Nottingham, some consisting of notes made by visitors such as Daniel Defoe, who in 1724 described Nottingham as 'one of the most pleasant and beautiful towns in England',[51] and John Leland during the sixteenth century, along with Lucy Hutchinson's memoirs of her husband who was governor of the town whilst the Parliamentarians held it during the Civil War.[52] However, Nottingham has been fortunate to have had antiquarians who have not only written of their own times, but also sought out to record information about the history of buildings present in their day and structures and features which had disappeared.

Perhaps the most notable of these antiquarians were Robert Thoroton, whose *History of Nottinghamshire* was published in 1677, and German born, but Nottingham resident for a number of decades, Dr Charles Deering, who wrote *Nottingham Vetus et Nova*, which was published in 1751 but written prior to 1749 when Deering died.

Of other writers who have produced histories of Nottingham, some wrote their own texts based on contemporary observations and understanding of the past, others published information from other sources which were never identified or no longer survive and so cannot be scrutinised, and some wrote down local knowledge and stories passed down the generations which were not necessarily accurate.

Some, notably Deering, produced accounts which were a combination of these.

Antiquarians are an important source of knowledge with regard to Nottingham's archaeology. By taking an interest in development within in the city they became aware of archaeological remains when they were encountered.

An antiquarian named Frederick Clements visited a number of caves in Nottingham during the late nineteenth and early twentieth century and drew sketches of them. Like many of those who visited the caves he attributed greater age and more fanciful functions than that which was probably true, but his records ensured some notes were made of a number of caves which have since been destroyed and which otherwise we would not know about.[53]

William Stretton of Lenton visited several caves, writing brief descriptions and sketching them. He also excavated a pottery and tile kiln on George Street in 1819. He produced a document entitled '*The Stretton Manuscripts: BEING NOTES ON THE HISTORY OF NOTTINGHAMSHIRE*' before his death in 1828, which was published in 1910. Again, his writings are open to interpretation because although he was enthusiastic in his pursuit of knowledge of the past, his work was undertaken at a time when methods of excavation were primitive, with a lack of understanding of stratigraphy.

James Shipman, a geologist with an interest in the past, visited sites of archaeological interest during the late nineteenth and early twentieth centuries. He was particularly interested in the medieval town wall, the subject of his book '*Notes on The Old Town Wall of Nottingham Being A Description of Some Recent Exposures of it*', which also featured other unconnected points of archaeological interest which he encountered around the time of his investigations of the wall. Shipman keenly observed work being undertaken for the construction of the Great Central Railway cutting in 1898–99, which ran from north to south through the middle of the city centre, with the railway station located where the Victoria Shopping centre now stands, during which sections of the wall, post-Conquest defensive ditch, caves (especially on the site of the Town Hall which had existed on Weekday Cross during the medieval period up until the eighteenth century) and other features were observed. He also investigated caves on the site of the former General Hospital, located immediately north of Nottingham Castle, the subject of his pamphlet entitled '*Excavations at the Nottingham General Hospital, the New Wing, Interesting Discoveries With a Plan*'. Another of his interests was investigating evidence for the documented medieval suburb of Whiston, thought to have been located to the north of the modern Victoria Shopping Centre.

William Stevenson and Alfred Stapleton were two antiquarians writing in the late nineteenth and early twentieth centuries who produced general histories of the 'old town'. Their main interests were religious institutions, the subject of their monograph entitled '*The Religious Institutions of Old Nottingham.*' Stapleton was also author of '*Churches and Monasteries in Old and New Nottingham.*' He was also interested in market and boundary crosses, the subject of '*The Crosses of Nottinghamshire,*' Nottingham's caves, the subject of his book '*Nottingham Caves,*' and graveyards, with '*The Nottingham Graveyard Guide*' on the subject. Both Stapleton and Stevenson also wrote features in the Nottinghamshire Guardian answering the questions of correspondents with an interest in the past.

Amateur archaeology grew in the twentieth century. Key amongst the groups involved in the discipline was the Thoroton Society Excavation Section, later renamed the Nottingham Archaeological Society, which was formed in 1936 and led by George Campion in his role of Director of Fieldwork. Campion owned a motorcycle company started by his father, who was also engaged in amateur archaeology. George Campion took early retirement so that he could spend more time on his growing passion of archaeology which he had been involved in from around 1931.

His interest coincided with a period of redevelopment of the city which afforded opportunities for investigation of Nottingham's previously hidden past. The opportunities were only restricted by the onset of the Second World War which reduced the number of active members of the society as they took up National Service, although the

George Campion examining pottery in his pottery laboratory. (Courtesy of H. Houldsworth and www.picturethepast.co.uk)

bombing of some buildings in Nottingham resulted in eventual opportunities to investigate the caves beneath.

Some of those sites excavated by the Thoroton Society Excavation Section and Nottingham Archaeological Society include caves at Fisher Gate, caves at Bridlesmith Gate, the Drury Hill cave complex, the caves beneath the Salutation Inn, a cave on Castle Road beneath the castle and the Water Cave off Castle Boulevard, caves on the site of the Ice Stadium and the Flying Horse, a cave system at Fletcher Gate where a time capsule was buried by Campion in a well, and above ground excavations at the site of the former Grey Friar's burial ground, Western Street, Lister Gate, a site on Castle Boulevard and an excavation around the Castle Rock as well as other excavations and site visits elsewhere in Nottingham and Nottinghamshire.

George Campion and other members of the Thoroton Society Excavation Section during an excavation of a cave under 58 Castle Gate in March 1939. (Courtesy of George F. Campion and www.picturethepast.co.uk)

Campion was an enthusiastic amateur archaeologist who often risked his health and safety in pursuit of his hobby. On one occasion he swung on a rope to investigate a small passage leading into a cave on the Castle Rock. He also ventured into caves where there was a real risk that the cave roof would collapse on top of him and he reportedly lost his sense of smell after investigating a charnel pit on Milton Street which contained human bones covered in quicklime at its base.

Whilst many of Campion's conclusions are open to debate, and a number can be dismissed given information acquired since his work, the work carried out by the Thoroton Society Excavation Section and Nottingham Archaeological Society saw the real beginning of an understanding and interest in Nottingham's archaeology. Its work encouraged an interest amongst the wider public, in particular regarding Nottingham's man-made caves, because Campion wrote regular articles for the Nottinghamshire Guardian in which he described some of his most interesting discoveries, accompanied with imaginative reconstruction drawings which appealed to his readers' imaginations. Amongst these were depictions of pit cave dwellings and Saxon stables which were in all probability something quite different and not nearly as exciting, but interesting nonetheless. Campion continued his involvement in archaeology, visiting sites and assisting with occasional excavations, until shortly before his death in March 1955.

The Peverel Archaeological Group was born out of the Nottingham Archaeological Society following disagreements between members of that society. The details of the disagreements are unknown, with a member describing them only as 'internal dissention' which resulted in a quarter of the members deciding to form the breakaway group. It was founded in 1949 and consisted of many of the members of the Nottingham Archaeological Society, most notably George Campion's son-in-law, Herbert Houldsworth. Its main activities included the excavation of caves, notably at the castle and beneath the long gone Moot Hall Public House and Collin's Almshouses, and excavations at St Nicholas' church rectory and during the early work associated with the construction of Maid Marian Way. The group started to decline in activity in the mid 1950s and eventually merged with the Thoroton Society in 1960 when the Archaeological Section of the Society was formed. As professional archaeology began, the activities of the Archaeological Section went into decline.

Tony Wass had been a member of the Peverel Archaeological Group whilst at school, but also carried out work independent of the group. He carried out excavations predominately of caves threatened by development, sites on the projected line of the pre- and post-Conquest defences but also sites where he believed the 'southern defences' of the medieval town would be located. He was also responsible for an excavation where a large number of human skeletons were encountered, a site which is explored in detail in a later chapter. He maintained an active interest in archaeology until the mid-1960s.

In 1964 Alan MacCormick was appointed Keeper of Human History by Nottingham City Council. Early into his career in Nottingham Alan met Tony Wass who showed him around the city pointing out areas where Wass had excavated. This sparked a fascination with Nottingham's archaeology in Alan's mind, especially sites where caves had been investigated, and the interest has never waned. Alan continues to be involved in archaeology in Nottingham in his role as President of the Nottingham Historical and Archaeological Society.

The Society was founded in 1968 as a consequence of the building of the Broadmarsh Shopping Centre and the threat of destruction of the caves found during its construction. Today it carries out ongoing excavations of the Broadmarsh Centre caves. The valuable work of the Society helped secure the future of the cave complexes at the Broadmarsh Shopping Centre, which had been threatened by the development, and beneath 3–7 Middle Pavement, ensuring both systems were designated Scheduled Monuments, protected by law. Other notable caves excavated by the society include those beneath the former Barker's Coffee House (48–52 Bridlesmith Gate) and the caves encountered following the demolition of the Farmers Drapery store on South Parade and Cheapside.

The Nottingham Flying Squad was a group of amateur archaeologists who undertook small-scale excavations including at Chapel Bar where the town wall and ditch were encountered and a somewhat disastrous excavation at Fisher Gate during which much archaeology was destroyed. Key amongst the group was Bob Alvey who worked at the Nottingham University Museum and due to his position had a large amount of experience of Nottingham pottery.

The Hidden History Team, founded by Paul Nix, was also involved in the investigation of caves (most notably at Goose Gate) until the 1980s. Whilst some of their theories on the site are questionable (such as caves used for bear baiting), like the Nottingham Historical and Archaeological Society, they contributed to a greater appreciation of the caves by increasing awareness of them through promoting their activities in the press.

Unfortunately, the earliest amateur archaeologists and in particular antiquarians, did not always make detailed records of what they found or where they found it. The dates given to artefacts have also been shown to be wrong in some instances. For example, a token found on Wollaton Street was believed, by Campion, to date to the Iron Age[54] but was later shown to date to between the fourteenth and sixteenth centuries.[55] Where artefacts no longer exist it is uncertain whether Campion and others made similar errors which resulted in features being dated erroneously. This means that archaeologists now have to decide whether or not they can trust the accuracy of what was written. Additionally, interpretations made by those who worked in the past are sometimes questionable in light of knowledge gained more recently as a result of modern professional archaeological techniques and knowledge. Nonetheless, without these antiquarians and early amateur organisations we would have no knowledge of many pieces of evidence that have been lost as a result of development in the city and we have to be grateful that any records were made, and the groups and individuals existed, at all.

Professional Archaeology in Nottingham's Historic Core

Continual professional archaeological investigation in Nottingham began in 1969. Until 1992 when Planning Policy Guidance Note 16 (PPG16) was implemented there had been no expectation for archaeological work to be undertaken when development of a site took place. It had, until that year, been very much a matter of goodwill on the part of the landowner if fieldwork was undertaken.

Until PPG16 archaeology in Nottingham was largely the pursuit of amateurs who had an interest in the subject, academics and occasionally local authorities if the local authority had the resources, and councillors could be persuaded, to hire an archaeologist or, in rare cases, a small team of archaeologists. Professional archaeologists were often aided by volunteers and 'Borstal boys' from Lowdham Grange in the case of Nottingham, and some staff were employed under job creation schemes, during big excavations, particularly in the 1980s.

As a result of the construction of the Broadmarsh Shopping Centre, and the concerns of many members of the public regarding the impact of its construction on the historic environment, Charles Young was hired by the city council to undertake a rescue excavation and salvage as much information as possible, using professional techniques. It had long been recognised that land off Drury Hill should have been on the projected line of the defensive ditch of the pre-Conquest, late-Saxon borough. In fact, towards the beginning of the twentieth century the antiquarian William Stevenson had established a theory that the pre-Conquest defensive ditch ran around the western, northern and eastern extent of the Lace Market (or St Mary's Hill as it was known at the time). This theory was created by studying the topography of the area and the layout of the streets, which were not consistent with the rest of the city and were therefore believed to be of great antiquity with the outlying streets of the Lace Market respecting a boundary of some sort.[56] Subsequent antiquarian and amateur archaeological excavations showed that the theory was correct. It was therefore a reasonable assumption that the ditch and possibly associated features and evidence of occupation would survive at Drury Hill.

Between 1969 and 1980 six of these big 'rescue archaeology' excavations were undertaken by Nottingham City Museums Field Archaeology Section, funded by the Department for the Environment. The responsibility for such work has subsequently passed to English Heritage. These excavations were carried out predominantly in the Lace Market, with an excavation at Goose Gate aimed at uncovering evidence of the spread of occupation after the Norman Conquest. The Lace Market is where it was believed the earliest activities in the city took place and development here provided the opportunity to investigate Nottingham's origins.[57] These excavations transformed our knowledge of Nottingham's past, and since writing this book an English Heritage funded project has commenced, with work being undertaken by Trent & Peak Archaeology, in partnership with Nottingham City Council, to better understand what was found during the excavations.

Each of the 'Big Six' excavations, as they are affectionately known, will be discussed throughout the following chapters in relation to the excavated evidence which has contributed to our knowledge of many different aspects of Nottingham's past. The first was at Drury Hill, where the easternmost extent of the Broadmarsh Shopping Centre currently stands. The excavations were undertaken between August 1969 and January 1971 in advance of the construction of the shopping centre. The second excavation took place on the north side of Woolpack Lane in 1970. Excavations on the north side of Fisher Gate, immediately south of the Ice Centre, were undertaken over the course of three seasons in 1971, 1973–74 and 1978–79. An excavation on the former Boots Garage site, located between Woolpack Lane and Barker Gate on land now occupied by the Ice Centre, was undertaken in 1972. The site was so named because it was owned by the Boots company

Area B of Halifax Place. Gordon Young is shown triangulating the northern edge of the Middle Saxon boundary ditch. (Nottingham City Museums and Galleries, NCMG 2013–4)

and to avoid any confusion with the Woolpack Lane site. Excavations on the north side of Goose Gate were undertaken between 1976 and February 1979. Finally, excavations at Halifax Place, on land bounded by Halifax Place, Pilcher Gate, High Pavement and St Mary's Gate, were undertaken between June 1978 and March 1980.[58]

Although PPG16 has now been superseded with the National Planning Policy Framework its principles remain the same. The relevant section of the Framework is headed 'Conserving and enhancing the historic environment' and it sets out to achieve this aim by recognising that the historic environment makes a positive contribution to society, the economy, culture and the environment. The impact of a proposed development on heritage assets must be considered when determining whether a planning application should be approved. It states that, 'Local planning authorities should set out in their Local Plan a positive strategy for the conservation and enjoyment of the historic environment…in doing so they should recognise that heritage assets are an irreplaceable resource and conserve them in a manner appropriate to their significance…'. When considering applications an applicant will be expected to describe the significance of any heritage assets affected, with the Historic Environment Record being consulted and appropriate expertise used. A desk based assessment and, if necessary, field evaluation should be required for sites with the potential to include heritage assets with archaeological interest. There is also a requirement for developers to 'record and advance understanding of the significance of any heritage assets to be lost (wholly or in part) in a manner proportionate to their importance' and make this information publicly accessible.[59]

Fieldwork is undertaken where it is felt a development will impact upon archaeological remains although the economic climate has meant little development taking place and consequently extremely little archaeological work in Nottingham. In the past a large number of professional field units have undertaken fieldwork in the historic core of Nottingham. These are Archaeological Project Services, Birmingham Archaeology, CgMS (formerly John Samuels Archaeological Consultants), Northamptonshire Archaeology, SLR Consulting, Trent & Peak Archaeology, the University of Leicester Archaeological Services and Wessex Archaeology.

At Garner's Hill where the Nottingham Contemporary Arts Centre now stands, only a stone's throw from Halifax Place, a series of watching briefs and excavations were undertaken by Trent & Peak Archaeology in 2005 and 2006. The site of Nottingham Ice Centre was subjected to evaluation, excavation and watching briefs by John Samuels Archaeological Consultants. Excavations and watching briefs have been undertaken at Nottingham Castle by Trent & Peak Archaeology, York Archaeological Trust, and SLR Consulting. The most recent archaeological work at the castle was in 2009. The most significant fieldwork at the castle was undertaken between 1976 and

1984, however, before PPG16. The site of the former General Hospital, located immediately north of the modern extent of the castle grounds but which included the most northerly part of the castle, were excavated between 1994 and 1997 by Trent & Peak Archaeology and the University of Leicester Archaeological Services.

Most archaeological work starts off at the planning application stage. The planning officers at the city council will pass on details of any planning applications for sites in any of the Archaeological Constraint Areas defined in the Local Plan/Local Development Framework for the city, to the City Archaeologist. The City Archaeologist will comment on any applications where archaeology might be encountered during the development, if it is permitted. If it is felt that archaeology may be encountered the developer will be asked to obtain a desk based assessment from a suitably qualified archaeological company, to assess what potential there is for archaeological deposits to be found on the site. This desk based assessment will then form part of the planning application and the City Archaeologist can advise the planners what mitigation strategies are required to account for any archaeology. Often no further work is necessary, but occasionally a watching brief is required in case any remains are disturbed during groundworks for the development. Less commonly it may be deemed necessary to undertake an evaluation to establish how likely it is that archaeology may survive, which is essentially a small scale excavation of part of the site. If the site is considered to have important archaeology a more extensive excavation will be necessary.

A Historic Landscape

The nature of Nottingham's geology, topography and natural features have defined its character and controlled its development. It has also produced unique difficulties for archaeological investigation.

The geology of the historic core is Nottingham Castle Sandstone (previously called Bunter Sandstone and Sherwood Forest Sandstone), a relatively soft sandstone with pebbles. This soft sandstone has enabled unique features to develop in the city over the course of at least 1150 years; man-made caves, the subject of a later chapter.

In most urban centres in this country archaeologists are fortunate to have deep deposits of material which provide evidence for a sequence of land use over a period of time. These deep stratified deposits also help preserve the earliest archaeological deposits and features because they are effectively better protected by being covered with more modern soils.

In most parts of the historic core of Nottingham, however, archaeologists have a problem in that during development and redevelopment of many sites during historic times, those undertaking development often stripped any deposits down to the sandstone bedrock before construction began. Thus any earlier soils and any artefacts contained within were removed, and sometimes used to fill pits, caves, or other holes in the ground, destroying what might otherwise have been a valuable record for archaeologists of what had taken place on that site in the past. As a consequence of the removal of layers of soil and other materials, on many sites only post medieval or modern deposits have been found. Nonetheless, due to the presence of sandstone bedrock, sites which have been stripped of their historic soils have often been found to contain features which are clearly discernable, being cut into the rock below.

The topography of the historic core consists of two raised areas of ground with the outcrop known as the Castle Rock being quite obvious, especially from Castle Boulevard, rising approximately 40m above street level. The site of the castle and the ground immediately north of it is raised above the rest of the historic core, which is precisely why it was an ideal site for the castle to be constructed. Those walking through the city today will find that from the Castle Rock the land gently slopes down towards the Old Market Square before quickly sloping upwards once again as soon as the Lace Market is entered. The Lace Market area itself is on a raised mound, which falls away towards Sneinton. It is no surprise that the Lace Market was also a focus of

The prominent outcrop of sandstone enabled Nottingham Castle to dominate the landscape during the medieval period. (The Author)

settlement and activity during the formative periods of Nottingham's development.

With the exception of the Castle Rock it is difficult for visitors to the city to realise that cliff lines exist within the city and one has to look harder for traces of the cliff line east of the castle. Yet until recent centuries the cliff was very much a feature of the historic core, especially around Cliff Road (known originally as Narrow Marsh), where there was a large drop down to the River Leen below with the Long Stairs and Malin Hill probably having some great antiquity to enable access to the Lace Market area from the river. This cliff, and in particular the drop of ground level, formed a natural obstacle to expansion. It can still be seen, from Canal Street in particular, but is partly obscured by buildings.

In 1931 Campion excavated a small area at the junction of Carrington Street and Canal Street, where he encountered the bed of a river.[60] Five years later Campion and the Thoroton Society Excavation Section excavated a site on the corner of Castle Boulevard and Wilford Road which revealed deposits of the same river indicating a deliberate filling of it, though no dating evidence for when this took place was found. The excavation recovered part of a small human skull with possible bullet hole, a sherd of pottery dating to c. 1700 and a layer of black mud containing organic material including from a poplar tree.[61]

Visitors to, and indeed even many residents of, Nottingham may be surprised to know that until the nineteenth century a river did flow along the southern boundary of the town where Castle Boulevard and Canal Street can now be found. It still flows but in the city it has been culverted. This river, called the River Leen, has its source in the Robin Hood Hills just outside Kirkby-in-Ashfield. It then flows through the grounds of Newstead Abbey, past Hucknall, through Papplewick, Bestwood Country Park, and then into Nottingham itself through Bulwell, Basford, Radford, and Lenton (meaning 'place on the Leen') before joining the River Trent opposite Wilford. The stretch of the river in the historic core was culverted in the nineteenth century and some of its braided channels were filled in, a fact shown by archaeological investigation.[62]

In 1975 an evaluation at Brewhouse Yard, to the west of the Waterworks Building, by Nottingham City Museums Field Archaeology Section revealed a channel of the Leen backfilled with nineteenth century material[63] and watching briefs between 1995 and 1996 on the former Boots Site on Island Street by Trent & Peak Archaeology noted the presence of in-filled channels of the Leen.[64]

With the canal having opened in the late eighteenth century, the river was superfluous. Towards the end of its use it was highly polluted and this, along with overcrowding in the slum areas such as Narrowmarsh, led to serious outbreaks of cholera from 1831. It was necessary to prevent it from being used as a source of drinking water and the only way to achieve this was to cover it.

In earlier times the Leen formed the main natural waterway and water source for the historic core of Nottingham and acted as a natural southern defence for the post-Conquest town. There is no indication of it in the historic core, however, with even the street once known as Leenside now being part of Canal Street.

It has been suggested that the river was diverted following the compilation of the Domesday Book because it fails to make reference to any mill on the river near the Castle Rock even though mills were known to have existed on the Leen at the base of the Castle Rock during the medieval period. It has been widely written that William Peveril, son of William the Conqueror who became the first Lord of Nottingham, diverted the river soon after the conquest so that it flowed closer to the Castle Rock in order to power the corn mills.[65] However, there is no archaeological evidence to show when a diversion took place, if it ever did.

In 1880 work was undertaken in the yard at the rear of the Red Lion Inn, which stood on London Road, revealing a 'perfect arch of the old Leen Bridge.'[66] In 1969, during Gas Board excavations on Canal Street, an arch of a bridge consisting of large stones carved 'V & T' was found by Alan MacCormick. It was believed to date to the eighteenth century.[67]

The arches found in 1880 and 1969 were indeed parts of the Leen bridge which formed the main route crossing the river, with its causeway known as Flood Road and now named London Road. The Reverend James Orange, in his book 'History and Antiquities of Nottingham,' published in 1840, wrote that the entrance to the bridge was at the rear of the Red Lion.[68]

The Leen Bridge was known as 'the town bridge' on account of its upkeep being the responsibility of the townspeople and was located on the site of the present London Road. The area at the town end of the bridge was known as Bridge End and was first mentioned in 1362, showing that a bridge was at this location at that time.[69] It is quite likely, however, that the bridge was considerably older than the fourteenth century.

Beneath Flood Road were a number of arches and culverts bridging pools and marsh land, part of which was known as the Chainy Bridges. The earliest reference to the 'Cheany Brygges' was in 1485 or 1486.[70] In 1809 the foundation of nine culverts was laid and the Chainy Pool Arch built.[71]

There were several rebuilds of the bridge due to flooding, general disrepair and because part of the bridge was demolished during the Civil War to prevent a Royalist siege of the town.[72] In 1796, following a major flood which destroyed the previous bridge, a seven-arch bridge was built.[73]

The area around the Leen was, in historic times, marshland and as a result there are deeper deposits there. Whilst it is believed little activity took place south of the River Leen, outside the medieval town in the area known as The Meadows, it is thought the area immediately north of the river, around Cliff Road and Canal Street, could still have preserved remains associated with the tanning industry. However, there are difficulties in excavating in such areas because of the high water table. During trial trench excavations on Canal Street by Northamptonshire Archaeology the trenches flooded rendering it impossible to excavate to the depth where archaeological deposits are likely to be.[74]

From medieval, and possibly even Saxon, times a bridge crossed the River Trent, forming the main access route to the historic core from the south via Flood Road and the Leen Bridge. It was possibly first alluded to in 920 in the Anglo-Saxon Chronicle, which refers to the building of a bridge to link Nottingham with a settlement at the south, which has been presumed to be West Bridgford, and was known as the Hethbeth Bridge (and derivatives of that name) in medieval times.[75]

The bridge had a chapel, dedicated to St James, which will be discussed in a later chapter, from the fourteenth to sixteenth or seventeenth century for the benefit of travellers wishing to give thanks for a safe passage.[76] It was quite common to have chapels near entrances to towns and in particular close to or on bridges. Indeed the Leen Bridge had a chapel dedicated to St Mary at its town end.[77]

The bridge was often in need of repair throughout its existence, largely due to flooding or erosion. In 1683 the flooding was so severe that the bridge was almost totally destroyed. As a result the largely timber bridge was rebuilt in stone with twenty arches to increase its strength.[78] The bridge was rebuilt again further east of the medieval bridge in 1871 and widened in 1926 to form the current Trent Bridge.[79] Part of the former bridge can still be seen today and is protected as a Scheduled Monument, at the southern most end of the old bridge, in West Bridgford.

The River Trent itself was a primary reason for the establishment of a settlement at Nottingham. The river has always been navigable and the lay of the land provided a ford at this location.[80]

In 1937 the digging of foundations of the former Postal Sorting Office on Huntingdon Street South, which were observed by Campion, revealed the course of a small stream.[81] In 1980 a watching brief by Nottingham City Museums Field Archaeology Section took place on Huntingdon Street during the demolition of houses and excavation of machine-dug trenches. Below relatively modern levelling layers of soil, a dark silt layer was identified and interpreted as the bed of the same stream found by Campion.[82] The stream was known about from a mass of historic sources including documentation and maps. It was culverted during the nineteenth century and was known as The Beck.

The Beck was a stream or brook flowing at the east of the historic core of Nottingham with its source at St Ann's Well. It ran under St Ann's Well Road and flowed towards the River Leen, with the confluence close to Island Street. It has been speculated that the Beck formed a natural defence for the post-Conquest town.[83] St Ann's Well is itself an interesting feature and more than just a source of drinking water. The well, the earliest reference to which dates to 1301,[84] consisted of a rock cut chamber in which people could immerse themselves in flowing water: the water was reputed to have healing properties. It had a ceremonial function and once a year the mayor and aldermen of the town would follow a procession to the well, led by musicians. This procession first began in 1601 and continued until the outbreak of Civil War.[85] The well was covered in tiles, at least during the post-medieval period.

Shipman's observations during the excavation of the Great Central Railway cutting showed dark organic deposits suggestive of the area having been flooded due to both the Beck flooding and also that the post-Conquest town ditch had acted as a drain and flooded near St John's Hospital, due to the lay of the land there. Shipman thought a pool was formed by the Beck at the north east of the town.[86]

Shipman also found evidence of associated features. Towards the end of the nineteenth century during groundworks just north of Perth Street stone slabs were encountered in line with the Beck. Shipman thought the stones to be a boundary for the Beck. There was also evidence of a wooden causeway 2ft (0.6m) above the stones.[87]

Excavations between 1932 and 1959 revealed evidence for another waterway, which is little known of, but which played a small role in medieval times.

In 1932 to 1933 an excavation by Campion was carried out in advance of the construction of the Ritz cinema, as it was then known, where the Odeon building stood off Maid Marian Way until it was very recently demolished. An 'old' water gulley was excavated, running approximately east to west through the centre of the site.[88]

In 1933 test pits were excavated by Campion to a depth of 14ft (4.3m) on a site at the junction of the former Stanford Street and Grey Friar Gate. The pits revealed gravel at the bottom and a 2ft (0.6m) depth of water.[89]

In 1938 development work was undertaken at Lister Gate, which was observed by Campion and members of the Thoroton Society

Excavation Section. A water gully was found to have run down the slope of the street, which Campion believed was for draining the Derby Road hills to the meadows and marshes, although no evidence was uncovered for which area was being drained because too small an area was excavated to establish the route of the water course.[90]

In 1957 during the extension of a shop on Castle Gate, a 'cursory' examination was made by Tony Wass of the congregational burial ground into which the shop was to be extended. Contractors excavated a test pit in the south-east corner of the burial ground and revealed a gravel bed at 17ft (5.2m) depth. Within the gravel were sherds of water worn medieval pottery and bone fragments.[91]

Two years later Wass observed groundworks on the north-east corner at the eastern end of Castle Gate, following demolition of buildings and during the digging of new foundation trenches a feature identified as a former water channel was identified.[92]

It would appear the feature seen by Wass in 1957 and 1959 was, as he believed, the Rowell, the earliest reference to which is 1265.[93] It is my opinion that Campion's observations of the old gully were also the Rowell. Shipman had drawn a projection of the Rowell on the plan of the town in his 1899 book regarding the town wall, but no source was given for his information so it is uncertain whether or not he too saw this feature.

The Rowell was a small watercourse which acted as a drain through the historic core, running into the Leen and which formed a boundary between the St Peter and St Nicholas parishes. It is possible it may have been a man-made drain rather than a natural stream, though this is uncertain. It may have been natural but modified during its use. Certainly the area around the Rowell, notably St Peter's Square and Lister Gate, had been a marshy area during the medieval period. It is possible the Rowell was a means of attempting to reduce the waterlogged conditions.

In 1787 it was recorded that a stone obelisk was to be built over the Rowell at the bottom of Wheeler Gate, implying that it was still an open channel until at least that time, although no historic maps show its presence perhaps due its relatively minor importance.[94]

The Beginnings of a City

N ottingham's roots can be traced back thousands of years with some tentative evidence for prehistoric activity in the historic core.

A number of residual solitary artefacts or assemblages of artefacts (referred to by archaeologists as findspots) have been identified, predominantly during the Victorian period. With such a significant number of artefacts represented it would seem likely that there was a human presence in the historic core of Nottingham during the Bronze Age and possibly also the Neolithic period. It should be pointed out here that many of the findspots have only vague details regarding location and it has to be considered that the dates given to some of the artefacts may be wrong, with them dating to a different period altogether. Our knowledge has increased tremendously in recent decades and so unless the artefacts have been made available for modern analysis their dates are sometimes questionable. However, some of the more important artefacts were dated by professionals, sometimes at the British Museum or at least at the University of Nottingham. This is in contrast to some of those artefacts identified by the amateur archaeologists and antiquarians of yesteryear who did not always have the necessary skills and experience to provide accurate information. One has to occasionally keep an open mind about such interpretations and not place too much emphasis upon them.

One would expect prehistoric activity close to a major river such as the River Trent and certainly there is extensive evidence for it across much of the Trent Valley. It is therefore no surprise that the southern entrance to the historic core of Nottingham is not without its share of prehistoric artefacts.

During the early twentieth century a polished stone hammer was found close to the River Trent which, it is believed, dated to the Neolithic or early Bronze Age.[95] In 1930 a looped and socketed spearhead was 'fished-up' from the River Trent at Trent Bridge[96] and in 1956 a Bronze Age sword was dredged from the riverbed at West Bridgford, near Meadow Lane.[97]

Within what was the medieval town itself, a Neolithic or early Bronze Age sandstone axe head was found on the site of the Moot Hall public house, which once stood on Friar Lane, during or before July 1926 and was donated to Nottingham Castle Museum.[98] In 1883, during the building of the Great Northern and Great Central railway station (now the site of the Victoria Shopping Centre) on Charlotte Street, just north of the medieval defences, a large Neolithic stone axe and axe hammer were found.[99] Residual Neolithic flint implements have also occasionally been found in the backfill of caves.

A Middle Bronze Age palstave (a form of early axe) and a Late Bronze Age socketed axe were found at Chapel Bar, although the precise location and circumstances of their discovery are unknown.[100]

During groundworks for the construction of the Theatre Royal in 1865, a bronze axe, a bronze spearhead, and sword blade were found, all believed to date to the Bronze Age.[101]

Just north of the medieval town, occupation or activity was also evident in prehistoric times. In 1860 an assemblage of damaged Bronze Age implements were found in 'a heap' at Great Freeman Street. The metal work was found at a depth of just over 1m, and was thought to date to the late ninth or eighth century BC. It may have been an old hoard of implements gathered for recasting, a task which was never completed.[102]

In 1958, a Bronze Age barbed and tanged flint arrowhead was found in 'The Mounts', Sneinton, east of the medieval town, suggesting the possibility of prehistoric activity to the east of Nottingham.[103] However, the presence of one arrowhead is not conclusive because it could have been transported in soils stripped from one area and moved to Sneinton.

The nature and extent of the Neolithic and Bronze Age occupation and activity is unknown. It may be significant that the evidence was found outside the medieval defences, largely to the north and south, where development had been minimal until the Victorian period. Perhaps activity and even occupation had taken place in the void between the findspots, but had been destroyed by development over the course of thousands of years. Although there are no features relating to those periods it does seem a realistic possibility that people lived in Nottingham's historic core during the Bronze Age at least, even if only for a short period of time.

What is slightly more apparent in the traces of Nottingham's past, however, is occupation and activity during the Iron Age. Excavations at Fisher Gate revealed a gully with sherds of possible Iron Age pottery within the fill. The presence of sufficient amounts of residual pottery of the same type along with more recent pottery in deposits used to fill later features suggested Iron Age activity on the site with Iron Age deposits used to fill more recent holes in the ground.[104] It was Charles Young's opinion that there had been an 'Iron Age farmstead' that continued in use into the third century,[105] but there was insufficient evidence to test this conclusion because later activity on the site had destroyed any other Iron Age evidence that there might have been. Certainly it would appear some form of Iron Age occupation had taken place.

During the Halifax Place excavations cylindrical pits were discovered, cut into the rock. Sherds of Late Iron Age pottery, albeit small in number, were found within the fills of one of the pits, suggesting to the excavators that the pits dated to that period. One interpretation is that they were part of a Late Iron Age farmstead and were used for the storage of grain, but there was insufficient evidence for this. Indeed there is insufficient evidence to prove they even dated to the Iron Age period, with so much residual pottery around. No other features or deposits associated with this period were found. However, if Iron Age activity and occupation had not taken place in the area there would not have been so much residual pottery.[106]

Excavations on the site of the former General Hospital by University of Leicester Archaeological Services revealed a small section of prehistoric ditch measuring at least 2.20m wide (the full width could not be excavated) and 1.02m deep. It was thought to possibly be part of a circular ditch, though not enough of it was excavated to prove this. Sherds of probable late Iron Age pottery and struck flint in the ditch fill suggested a late Iron Age date for the ditch.[107]

During excavations of the Middle Bailey defences at Nottingham Castle by Chris Drage, sherds of Iron Age pottery and flint implements were found beneath a floor deposit, further suggesting an Iron Age presence on the Castle Rock which would be sensible given its prominent position in the landscape.[108]

Residual Iron Age pottery has been found elsewhere in the historic core. The most likely explanation for residual material is when soils dating to the Iron Age, containing Iron Age artefacts, were stripped away and moved around, eventually being used to fill in features from a later time. Residual artefacts are encountered on almost every archaeological site and can cause confusion in the dating of deposits and features but generally a feature can be approximately dated using the most recent artefacts in each layer of soil or other material and using other deposits and features to establish a relationship. So if you can establish a layer dates to the tenth century then the layer and any features below it must also be tenth century or older.

It is certain therefore that there was Iron Age occupation and activity of an unknown nature on the highest points of the historic core; the Lace Market and on the Castle Rock. Its full extent can sadly not be assessed.

Excavations have failed to locate any features, structures or substantial deposits associated with the Roman period within the historic core of Nottingham. This is not to say they never existed, for it could well be that later development destroyed any such evidence, but it would hint at the likelihood that any occupation or activity was limited. Nonetheless evidence for occupation or activity has been located in the form of residual pottery on several sites in sufficient quantities to show the Romans may have had some presence.

During the construction of a gasometer at the east end of Island Street in 1840, remains of a well preserved oak tree, a stag's horn, a deer skull, a tooth up to eight inches long, human bones, an alleged Roman denarius, fragments of two 'Roman' urns and a pewter jug were found.[109] If the antiquity of the artefacts was correctly established, then this could be further evidence for Roman activity.

Nonetheless, it was the Saxon period which has left the most tangible evidence of the beginning of a continual occupation of the historic core. Sadly there is no evidence for early-Saxon activity or occupation, if activity or occupation took place during this period. However, from the Middle Saxon period onwards Nottingham makes its presence known to us.

Snotenceham

Continuous occupation in the historic core of Nottingham is believed to have begun during the Saxon period when a settlement which was to be known variously as Snotenceham, Snotengeham, Snothryngham and Snottingham, was founded. Excavations have provided evidence of one or more settlements in the historic core during this period and have provided some evidence for its development.

At Fisher Gate and Boots Garage excavations revealed the shallow remains of two near-parallel ditches running east to west approximately 150m apart. They were considered to be so similar in terms of shape and size that they were believed by Charles Young to be two sides of an enclosure ditch.[110] However, given the close proximity of the sections of ditch at Boots Garage and Fisher Gate it is possible they are related. The fill of the ditches contained Iron Age and mid-Saxon pottery, suggesting a Middle Saxon (c. 650–850) date. If indeed both ditches are related they are thought to represent the northern and southern boundaries of a Middle Saxon enclosed settlement. The ditch is not thought to have been defensive due to the poor military siting, being on lower ground to that immediately to the west, and there was no evidence of a bank or rampart.[111] All that can be proven is that the eastern part of the Lace Market was occupied during the Middle Saxon period but the nature, and extent, of that occupation is uncertain.

The ditch did not extend west of Bellar Gate and Belward Street because if it did it would have been seen cut into the rock, when a watching brief took place in the 1980s, and it is thought that any settlement, if it existed, may have had the Beck as a natural eastern boundary.

Yet if the settlement existed and there was a ditch around it, where is the western side of that ditch? Given the small stretches of ditch it is dangerous to say there was a ditch which ran from Fisher Gate and linked up to that at the Boots Garage site. There may not have been any such enclosed settlement.

It would certainly appear that the ditches were Middle Saxon and so activity and occupation of that date was present in the eastern side of the historic core, but there is little further evidence for it. There has never been any evidence identified for structures or any other features dating to this period. The sherds of a single Ipswich Ware pitcher found on the site of the Ice Centre, during fieldwork by John Samuels Archaeological Consultants, in advance of the construction of the Ice Centre, forms the only artefact and evidence of Middle Saxon occupation between the two ditches.[112] Any other evidence may have been destroyed during development of the site during the medieval, post-medieval and modern periods, such as when the original ice stadium was built.

A pamphlet produced in 1983 implies that Middle Saxon occupation was confined to that area on the east of the historic core close to the Beck.[113] The plan showing this early ('Period One') 'settlement', has been widely reused in various publications and has been relied upon in many pieces of research. Unfortunately it is not quite accurate.

Excavations at Halifax Place proved there was occupation during the Middle Saxon period further west than the Period One settlement. A rock cut ditch, probably acting as a boundary ditch, was found on the site, extending approximately 30m in length, and it continued beyond the area excavated so its full length is unknown. It too contained Middle Saxon pottery and was believed to date to the period of c. 650–850, though when exactly in this period it was created is unknown. Certainly it had fallen out of use and was filled in by the late Saxon period (c. 850–1066).[114] This would imply that if the Fisher Gate and Boots Garage ditch comprised one enclosed settlement, that there was a second settlement, enclosed or otherwise, on the higher land at Halifax Place, close to where St Mary's church was later built. It is possible that two or more areas of separate occupation existed at the same time but it is also possible that a settlement at the east of the historic core, if such a settlement existed on the low land near to the Beck, fell out of use and that a new settlement was founded on the higher land at a later time still within the Middle Saxon period recognising that the Period One settlement was in a poor location. Either way, occupation in the Middle Saxon period was far more extensive than the 1980s pamphlet suggests with two areas of occupation existing at the western and eastern ends of the pre-Conquest, late-Saxon borough (the level of occupation and/or activity, if any such existed, in between the two is currently unknown).

It could be that one of these early areas of occupation was occupied by Saxons until shortly before the arrival of the Vikings.

Nottingham's Viking connections are little known. Vikings were first recorded in Nottingham in 868 when they wintered there. The Anglo-Saxon Chronicle records: 'A.D. 868. This year the same army went into Mercia to Nottingham [the name Nottingham is simply a translation; the town was not known as Nottingham until much later], and there fixed their winter-quarters; and Burhred king of the Mercians, with his council, besought Ethered, king of the West-Saxons, and Alfred, his brother, that they would assist them in fighting against the army. And they went with the West-Saxon army into Mercia as far as Nottingham, and there meeting the army on the works, they beset them with-in. But there was no heavy fight; for the Mercians made peace with the army.'[115]

It is quite possible that the dating evidence is slightly wrong and that the ditches thought to be Middle Saxon (650-850) could in fact date to 868 and represent the 'works' of the winter quarters or that the Vikings used pre-existing boundary ditches created by the Saxons.

Five years after the first Vikings arrived, in 873, a Scandinavian settlement was recorded in Nottingham. By this time the defences presumably ran to the full extent of the pre-Conquest borough which was coterminous with the modern day Lace Market because the pre-Conquest ditch has been found to date to this period. Between 877 and 918 Nottingham was one of the five Boroughs of the Danelaw; Nottingham, Leicester, Derby, Stamford and Lincoln each had a fortified settlement under the rule of the Danes. It was an important settlement. In 918 Edward the Elder is recorded as having recaptured the town from the Danes and strengthened its defences, probably increasing the size of the ditch and creating a rampart. The defences consisted of a ditch on the west, north and east sides, with the cliff line forming a natural southern boundary and a rampart beside the ditch.[116] Two years later Edward founded a second settlement to the south, believed to be West Bridgford, although it could have been Wilford, which was connected to Nottingham by a bridge.[117]

The town fell to the Norse in 939 and was recaptured by the Saxons for the final time in 942.[118] Thus for a period of approximately eight decades Nottingham had a Viking presence and it is likely its influence continued following the recapture by the Saxons.

Unfortunately, little archaeological evidence directly relating to Viking occupation survives. Nonetheless the archaeology does reveal important evidence to show Nottingham's Viking associations.

In 1851 work was undertaken to create a pleasure ground on the east side of the historic core, outside the medieval town. Although the precise location is unknown, notes which survive recorded the work as having been carried out 'in a field adjoining the new baths and wash-houses outside the town.' Other records state it took place in a field between St Mary's Cemetery (there were three cemeteries belonging to St Mary's; the one referred to was the one located on Bath Street) and the County Lunatic Asylum. It would therefore appear that the work was associated with the construction of buildings now belonging to Victoria Leisure Centre.[119]

At a depth of a little over 3ft (0.91m), 'two skulls and other human remains' were noted as having been found. Upon full excavation it was shown that the skeletons represented two individuals who had been buried with grave goods consisting of parts of two iron swords and a spearhead. One of the swords was almost complete, but broken in two, and is believed to date to c. 900–950. It measured 91cm in length. The spearhead is believed to date to the ninth century and may be an import from the Carolingian Frankish Empire or a local copy and similar examples have been found in London and York. It

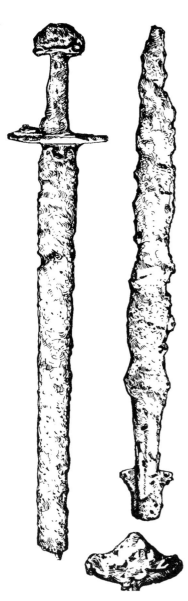

Drawings of the Viking artefacts found in Nottingham in 1851. (Reproduced from the Victoria County History)

measured 62cm in length. Also present was a sword pommel of late-Saxon type. This type of pommel was in use during the ninth century but continued in use to the end of the Anglo-Saxon period. Other examples have been found in Abingdon and Lincoln. One of the sword blades had signs of an inscription, but what was written, if it could be made out at the time of discovery, is unknown.[120]

The presence of grave goods and their age has raised the suggestion that the two individuals were Vikings. The weapons are currently in storage at the Royal Armouries in Leeds simply because the Royal Armouries inherited the Tower Armouries collection, where the finds were originally sent, due to there not being a museum in Nottingham in 1851.

Were these two burials isolated or do they represent part of a hitherto unknown more extensive burial ground, which may have been destroyed or may remain undiscovered? It is possible that the skeletons represent two deaths during what was only ever a short stay during the winter of 868/869 when Vikings camped in Nottingham. If this is the case it is quite conceivable there would be no further burials in the immediate vicinity of the leisure centre. However, the dating evidence of the weapons accompanying the human remains renders this unlikely, if the weapons have been correctly dated, with the burials representing two men who lived and died during the Viking occupation.

The Vikings are known to have settled in

Nottingham by 873, creating a more permanent base until it was recaptured by Edward the Elder in 918, and then once more prior to 942 when it was again recaptured by the Saxon King Edmund from the Norse.[121] The likelihood is that the burials represent Scandinavian settlers, most probably from Denmark.

During the period of occupation between 873 and 918 there would have been many more burials than the two found in 1851, but the location of this early burial ground is unknown.

Efforts have been made to find any more burials; watching briefs were undertaken by Trent & Peak Archaeology in 1995 and 1996 on Bath Street, close to the Leisure Centre, in case further human remains might be encountered. However, nothing of archaeological interest was observed during the groundworks.[122]

It has been said that when Edward the Elder recaptured the town in 918 he strengthened the defences. There does appear to be archaeological evidence for this.

Whether it was the Vikings or Saxons who created the original extent of the pre-Conquest borough, coterminous with the present day Lace Market, defined by the defences, is unknown.

Antiquarian records from c. 1890 onwards provide evidence of the pre-Conquest defences, which has been further enhanced by archaeological investigations particularly during and since the 1960s. These excavations showed the defences consisted of a ditch with a relatively flat base and sides sloping 45-55 degrees with a rampart. The evidence suggests the defences were indeed strengthened following one of the recaptures of the town from the Vikings and that they were quickly abandoned and the ditch filled following the Norman Conquest.

In c. 1890 a stretch of the ditch was found between Carlton Street and Warser Gate during the excavation of foundations for a new warehouse. It was found to be 20ft (6.1m) wide and 20ft (6.1m) deep. A 'ditch dwelling' was found cut into the sandstone. It certainly seems that a cave was hewn into the side of the ditch whilst the ditch was empty, though whether or not the cave was a home remains uncertain.[123]

In 1911 the pre-Conquest ditch was encountered on a site between

Bridlesmith Gate and Fletcher Gate, possibly where King John's Arcade now stands.[124]

These excavations, and a study of the street patterns of the Lace Market, allowed Stevenson to plot his hypothesised course of the late-Saxon defences which provided a basis for further investigation.

Excavations by the Peverel Archaeological Group in 1957 at Bridlesmith Gate, between the Gate Inn and Tokenhouse Yard, revealed a 5m width of the pre-Conquest ditch (only part of the width was revealed due to heavy rain causing the risk of trench sides collapsing). The ditch had been deliberately filled with sandy material and there was evidence it had been previously cleaned out of material which had over time partly filled in. By clearing this material out of the ditch it once again became a better defensive feature. This probably took place when the defences were strengthened, with the deliberate filling taking place soon after the Norman Conquest but there was no dating evidence to prove this.[125]

In February 1961 a small hole was dug during alterations to a shop on the south west corner of Carlton Street. A small section of southern edge of the pre-Conquest ditch was exposed and recorded by Tony Wass. There was no dating evidence in the fills of the ditch.[126]

That same year Wass excavated at the Black Swan Public House on Goose Gate where he once again encountered the ditch. Wass' notes refer to a human cranium within the ditch and a human femur is shown in the ditch on a sketch plan but no further details were provided.[127] Wass' work suggests he was somewhat reticent about recording, especially in the public domain, the discovery of human remains, no doubt because of the sensitive nature of the work. This will become particularly apparent in a later chapter.

These excavations allowed Wildgoose to create a new plan of the projection of the ditch, based upon Stevenson's study and excavations which had taken place during the subsequent 49 years.[128]

Back at the Gate Inn on Bridlesmith Gate, in 1964, following its demolition, a small stretch of the pre-Conquest ditch was found, running north to south, parallel with Bridlesmith Gate. No dating evidence for the ditch was found. The surviving depth was 13ft 6 inches (4.1m) and its width was 28ft (8.5m). Again it was clear it had been quickly filled with sand at the end of its use.[129]

Excavations at Drury Hill revealed that the pre-Conquest ditch had cut through the remains of a building with possible sunken floor dated to no earlier than c. 850. This shows the area was occupied before the ditch was created.[130]

Excavations at Woolpack Lane corroborated this by revealing evidence for the ditch have been originally formed in the second half of the ninth century, suggesting it was possibly created during the Viking occupation, and was re-cut in the first half of the tenth century. This re-cut probably represents evidence for the strengthening of the defences under the instruction of Edward the Elder in 918, or possibly after 942 when King Edmund retook the town from the Norse.[131]

A watching brief at The Fountain public house on Bridlesmith Gate by University of Leicester Archaeological Services revealed a section of the ditch but no dating evidence was recovered. There was no evidence of a rampart found.[132]

So it would appear the Vikings either created or utilised a defensive ditch. It is my belief that the pre-Conquest borough, known as the Saxon borough, was in fact first created by the Vikings who dug a ditch marking the extent of their settlement and defending it from attack. They were attacked and the defences were strengthened but remained on the same line as those created by the Scandinavians who went on to take control once more of the town before it was finally regained by the Saxons just over a century before England fell to William the Conqueror. Although the Saxon borough remained independent within the wider medieval town, perhaps under the instruction of the Norman conquerors, the ditch was filled in.

The pre-Conquest borough's character is partially retained by the street pattern of the present day Lace Market, with much of the street patterns surviving to the present day. In fact, with the exception of the Ice Centre and the Broadmarsh Centre, much of the street pattern can be traced back to 1609 when the Sherwood Forest Survey plan of the town was produced[133] and many of the streets are known from documentary sources to have existed in medieval times. It is likely that most of the street pattern has remained constant since Saxon times, although of course streets have been widened.

Some of the roads (such as High Pavement and Woolpack Lane) respect the line of the pre-Conquest defences inside the defences and acted as an intra-mural road. Stoney Street, which runs north to south through the centre of the Lace Market, acted as the main street leading to the north.

In addition to the boundary of Snotenceham, excavations have provided evidence of some of the buildings in existence and some of the activities undertaken during the late Saxon period.

The Domesday Survey records that by 1086 there were 191 houses in the pre-Conquest borough, forty-eight of which were the houses of merchants. The accuracy of this figure is debatable. Twenty-three houses are recorded as being built on the now filled pre-Conquest ditch.[134]

Excavations at Halifax Place showed that once the Middle Saxon ditch had ceased to be used and been filled in, timber buildings were constructed on the site, one of which was built partly on top of the filled ditch during the late Saxon period.[135]

Halifax Place is an important site which gained significance from the late Saxon period if not before. Evidence of a large timber building, thought to possibly have been a 'hall', was found in the form of holes in which timber posts had once stood in the eleventh century. Other important buildings were created during the Saxon and medieval period. A pottery kiln producing unique pottery (not believed to have been found anywhere in the country except at Halifax Place) was in operation at some point in time between 940 and 1000, if not slightly before, and is believed to have only been used to produce pottery for those on the site. It was clearly an important site with high status use and population during the late Saxon period but also possibly during the Viking occupation.[136]

A possible sunken floored hut was found built over the Middle Saxon ditch at Fisher Gate during the late Saxon period.

As already stated the pre-Conquest ditch had cut a possible sunken house at Drury Hill, which was dated to no earlier than c. 850. This shows the settlement may have existed without any defensive ditch until c. 850 at around the time of the Vikings arrival, suggesting the

Vikings created the ditch or that it was created in the hope of preventing a Viking invasion.[137]

During excavations at the Boots Garage site, on the Woolpack Lane frontage, traces of late ninth or early tenth century timber buildings were found, placing the buildings possibly into one of the Viking periods of occupation. The earliest building, of uncertain date, was constructed of wattle and daub and was destroyed by fire. Further buildings were built in the tenth and eleventh centuries and into the medieval period.[138]

An excavation by John Samuels Archaeological Consultants in 2001 at a site on the corner of Fletcher Gate and Warser Gate revealed a series of small rock cut pits or post holes, which may be evidence of at least one timber building close to the junction of Warser Gate and Fletcher Gate, probably during the mid tenth century.[139]

When doing archaeology we usually only find the foundations of a building or holes in the ground where there were post holes and beam slots. We have therefore only a ground plan of what these buildings would have looked like and it is difficult for many to understand what these buildings were truly like. We can make educated guesses in these instances but often if the archaeology is not properly excavated, not properly recorded, or if later development has destroyed part of the archaeology, our information is incomplete. Due to the stripping of deposits down to the sandstone which often takes place in Nottingham there can be a large number of post holes in a small area, belonging to different buildings created at different times, overlapping one another. It is difficult to establish which post holes belong to which building. It is a case of joining the dots but sometimes errors can be made.

In addition to the physical remains of buildings or at least the holes that still exist where building materials had once been present, archaeologists can learn much about past occupation from looking at the contents of rubbish pits. We can learn what bowls and plates were used, what vessels were drunk from or used to store food and drink, sometimes bones of animals show what food was eaten and, if we are lucky, we may find tools, coins, jewellery or other items of luxury.

For example, during a watching brief at 14 Plumptre Street, by

Archaeological Project Services, Torksey type pottery dating to the late ninth to mid tenth century was found in pits believed to date to that period. Also found on the site, were a residual silver coin from the reign of Edward the Elder (899–925) and a rare Saxon pedestal lamp dating to the ninth century or earlier.[140]

In 1786, twenty coins dating to the mid eleventh century were found in Barker Gate and were believed to have been produced locally.[141] In 1880 a hoard of seventy-two coins from the reigns of Henry I (1100–1135) and Stephen I (1135–1154) was found in Rose Yard (the east side of Bridlesmith Gate, now occupied by King John's Arcade).[142] Unfortunately no further details were recorded for the coins but they may be evidence of a mint that existed from Saxon times up until possibly the early thirteenth century, coins from which have been found in hoards across the country.

The mint was first mentioned in 928, during the reign of Athelstan, when a grand synod declared that each town should be allowed to mint its own coins but places deemed important, such as Nottingham, were entitled to two or more moneyers. The mint may have existed before 928. One coin found, which was made in Nottingham, fails to have the portrait of Athelstan yet dates to his reign. After the synod it was a requisite that all coins should bear the king's portrait. The precise location of the mint in Nottingham is unknown and has been open to great speculation.[143]

Despite having two moneyers, it is thought that the Nottingham mint was of relatively minor importance during the period of its use, with coin hoards across the country containing very few coins struck in Nottingham compared with the numbers from other mints. For example, approximately 15,000 coins were found in a hoard at Beaworth, dating to the reign of William the Conqueror, but only 18 of these came from Nottingham. No coins have been found dating from the reigns of Eadmund (939–946), Eadwig (959–959), Eadgar (959–975) and Eadweard (975–978). It was also inactive for a time after the reign of Stephen (1135–1154) but whether or not the mint was in production during these reigns is uncertain. Certainly the reign of King Stephen saw a period of great unrest in Nottingham, when historic texts state fires caused great destruction in the town.[144]

Where is the Castle?

Visitors to Nottingham castle are often disappointed not to see a fortified structure such as that which they have often viewed in the numerous Robin Hood films and television programmes. Indeed today little survives of the once great medieval structure which was the pride of King Henry II and Richard III.

A late seventeenth-century Grade I Listed Building now stands on the site, which was granted to the city during the Victorian period and is now the property of Nottingham City Council. This was one of the homes of the Duke of Newcastle and now houses a museum and art gallery. The Ducal Palace is an important building in its own right, but there is naturally a great disappointment that its presence is at a cost to a building of potential greater importance. Indeed one small local organisation has attempted to campaign for the Ducal Palace to be demolished and rebuilt in Newcastle, with a castle based upon interpretations of what the medieval castle may have looked like, built in its place. To do so would be to remove a building of historic value to make way for an even more modern building which could mislead visitors further. The fact is we do not know what the medieval castle looked like because there were no contemporary illustrations of it, except for a basic stylised sketch used on the town seal and a stylised drawing on Speede's map of 1610. Perhaps it should be left as it is rather than attempt to create an artist's impression which will inevitably be deeply flawed. Another point to consider is that the castle evolved over time, expanding and being rebuilt, and so to recreate its appearance requires a snapshot of how it looked at only one part during its use over a period of almost six hundred years.

In 1617 an architect named John Smythson (sometimes spelt Smithson) drew a plan of the castle as it stood in that year.[145] The reason for this is unknown because the castle was unoccupied at the

A late seventeenth century Ducal Palace now stands on the site of the medieval Nottingham Castle. It was built to be the residence of the Duke of Newcastle but is now a museum and art gallery. (The Author)

time. Perhaps, because it was in disrepair, it was desired that it should be restored and so plans were drawn up to assess the condition. The work was never carried out, no doubt due to the extravagance of James I who preferred to spend money on his favourites, effectively bankrupting the country, and seemingly had little interest in Nottingham. He did visit Nottingham twice during his reign, in 1612 and 1614, but on these occasions he stayed at Thurland Hall (also known as Clare House), which stood on Pelham Street, due to the poor condition of the castle. Charles I also stayed at the Hall when he visited in 1634 and presumably also when he travelled to Nottingham to raise the Royal Standard.[146]

Whilst much of the castle has been destroyed, the gatehouse, curtain wall and small fragments of medieval masonry can still be seen but much of this was subject to restoration and modification in the early twentieth century. Part of the outer bailey bridge extending on to Castle Road (the outer end in Drage's opinion was destroyed by the eighteenth century) also survives.[147] However, for that which is not visible, archaeology has supplemented documentation to allow a greater understanding.

In 1904 excavations by members of the Thoroton Society were directed by F.W. Dobson who lived at 2 Castle Grove and whose garden contained the remains of one of the towers of the castle known as Richard's Tower on account of its construction during the reign of Richard III. The stone walls were found to be approximately 11ft (3.4m) thick. Part of a spiral staircase was uncovered, which was shown on the Smythson plan. It was believed at this time that the lower level of the tower had been used as a dungeon. The tower had been

A plan of Nottingham castle drawn by the architect John Smythson in 1617. Reproduced from Thoroton, 1797.

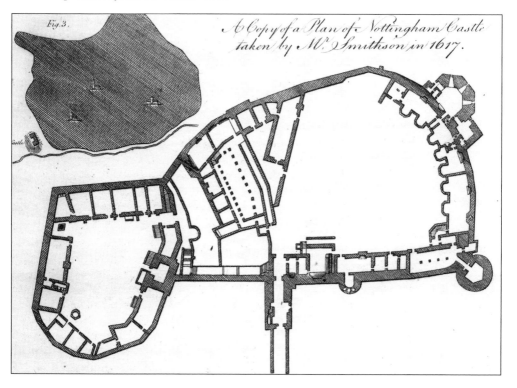

A medieval gatehouse, forming the entrance to Nottingham Castle. Although partly rebuilt in 1908 much of the original gatehouse still survives. (The Author)

filled in during the demolition of the castle in 1651. On the north side of the tower the base of a smaller attached tower was found.[148]

The excavation continued four years later, with the floor of the tower being encountered 18ft (5.5m) below ground level. The base of a pillar was found, as was a well which extended to a depth in excess of 50ft (15.2m), but a fireplace shown on the Smythson plan was not encountered, showing it had possibly been removed after 1617. There was no evidence to corroborate the theory that the tower had been used as a dungeon.[149]

Deposits outside the tower were associated with the demolition of the castle and landscaping in advance of the construction of the Ducal Palace. Dobson's excavation suggested that so much landscaping had taken place that the castle green was approximately 10–12ft (3–3.7m) higher than the medieval castle, which meant there was the chance that a substantial amount of the castle's foundations could have survived but was buried deep beneath the ground surface.[150]

Campion and the Thoroton Society Excavation Section continued where Dobson and others had left off. In 1936 they investigated Richard's Tower. They discovered that a doorway in the south-east corner led to a circular stone staircase. The well encountered by Dobson was found to be in excess of 120ft (36.6m) in depth. A vault was found to extend under the Richard's Tower and an adjacent smaller tower. A cave passage, known as the north-western passage or Davy Scot's Passage, was encountered and partially investigated. It could not be fully investigated because it was largely filled with debris. It was found to extend from the south-west building attached to Richard's Tower and down some steps, allegedly coming out in the Park on Ogle Drive. It was thought to have passed under the garden and building of 3 Castle Grove, before emerging from the cliff behind the garage.[151]

Campion et al also excavated the remains of a small tower to the east of Richard's Tower, at 1 Castle Grove. A stretch of the medieval castle wall was also encountered.

Part of the tower was excavated in 1950, by members of the Peverel Archaeological Group, though no details were recorded. They

H. Houldsworth excavating the Water Cave in 1938. (Courtesy of H. Houldsworth and www.picturethepast.co.uk)

excavated a number of caves on the castle grounds during the early 1950s but unfortunately very few details are available of their work at the castle, although a photograph shows the excavation of part of the filling of the Water Cave at the base of the Castle Rock. An excavation of Mortimer's Hole also took place.

Archaeological work at the castle only commenced in earnest during the 1970s. This was preceded by an infra red aerial survey and then complemented by geophysical work which showed some potential archaeological features.

Meanwhile, in 1976, Chris Drage and the Trent Valley Archaeological Research Committee (currently known as Trent & Peak Archaeology) had commenced excavations. That year the north-east tower, also known as the Black Tower, was partially excavated, as was part of the Middle Bailey curtain wall. When excavated further, Iron Age pottery, flint implements and part of what was believed to be the Middle Bailey ditch were encountered. The ditch was 10m wide and 5m deep and had been cut by Lenton Road. A rampart was found west of the North-East tower, with the ditch north of it.[152]

Richard's Tower was more thoroughly investigated and recorded than ever before and approximately 40m of curtain wall was excavated between Richard's Tower and the North-East tower. The Middle Bailey curtain wall was found to cut through the rampart showing that a wall replaced the earlier earthworks. During the twelfth or thirteenth

Excavation of the Black Tower under the direction of Chris Drage in March 1976. (Courtesy of George L. Roberts and www.picturethepast.co.uk)

century the ground level of the Middle Bailey was raised by approximately 2m, perhaps to enable better ground conditions for the substantial stone structures which made the castle. There was also evidence that the rock-cut ditch (sometimes referred to as a dry moat) had fallen out of use by the thirteenth century and that buildings to serve the castle were built over it. The North-East tower had been re-faced and evidence of alterations to the curtain wall were revealed as was evidence of the robbing some of the facing stones when the castle fell out of use. When the curtain wall was largely demolished part of its remnants were used as a foundation for a late seventeenth century boundary wall for the Ducal Palace, thus preserving it.[153]

Foundations of a clay-bonded stone medieval wall were found in the south-west corner of the Green, along with three post holes. It was thought a timber building with a stone base may have existed, possibly in the thirteenth century.[154]

A burial, believed to date to the time of the Civil War was also found here aligned east to west, as is the Christian custom. The burial was close to where we know, through documentation, the Common Chapel was located. The chapel was used as a hospital during the Civil War. The skeleton was reburied and it is quite possible there are other burials still undiscovered at the castle. A tibia from an individual aged between twelve and fourteen was found within a layer of sand used to raise the level of the Middle Bailey.[155]

There was evidence that the ground level of the Middle Bailey had been raised approximately 2m during the twelfth or thirteenth century, perhaps coinciding with the time that the timber castle was rebuilt with stone.[156]

The gatehouse and bridge were investigated and the bridge found to have once been fitted with a timber drawbridge. There was also a drawbridge within the castle grounds, in the Middle Bailey. This bridge was found to have been modified in the sixteenth century when stone arches were built either side of it.[157]

Three holes were excavated south of the Ducal Palace in the paved area next to the wall and railing along the cliff edge to make way for anchorage for abseiling. In two of the pits medieval masonry was found below thick deposits. At a depth of c. 50cm a layer of charcoal and ash was found, possibly created during the Chartists' arson attack on the Ducal Palace in 1831.[158]

A watching brief was undertaken at the courtyard of Nottingham Castle following the excavation of foundations for a new Ladies Toilet. The northern edge of a probable rock cut ditch was seen but it could not be investigated further.[159]

In 1994 an excavation was undertaken by York Archaeological Trust within the Ducal Palace in advance of the installation of a lift shaft. Only evidence relating to the landscaping of the site and construction and modification of the Ducal Palace was encountered. It is thought that the construction of the palace may have destroyed any evidence of the medieval castle within its footprint.[160]

On Christmas Day 1996 a large rock collapse took place at the Castle Rock, undermining part of a boundary wall south of the Ducal Palace which collapsed in turn, exposing two fragmented lengths of the same wall, which was found to be medieval in origin.[161]

During work for the extension of the Nottingham Castle lecture theatre, a length of stone wall was uncovered running at approximately a right angle to the Ducal Palace and had been damaged during the palace's construction and during later work in the nineteenth century. The wall, which was recorded by Gordon Young on behalf of the City Council, was thought to date to the reign of Henry II. Further evidence for landscaping after the medieval castle was demolished was also encountered.[162]

A watching brief was undertaken by Trent & Peak Archaeology during the excavation of trenches and test pits for cable installation, which generally went to a depth of 90cm. A trench running from the south west of the Green to the courtyard, revealed pits containing Saxo-Norman pottery, which may have been in use at the time of the earliest timber castle. Medieval deposits were found to survive at a depth of 0.5m below the tarmac surface around the western entrance of the Ducal Palace but were more deeply buried on the east side, probably due to extensive landscaping.[163]

Evidence suggesting there may have been a gate house earlier than that which stands today was found in the form of walls with a possible break, which do not feature on the Smythson Plan, located to the west of the gatehouse which still survives, but no dating evidence was found. It must be medieval, however, and predate the later gatehouse which is believed to date to the fourteenth century.[164]

There was evidence of widespread landscaping in the late seventeenth century, and levelling of the Middle Bailey ditch in the mid eighteenth century.[165]

A watching brief was undertaken again by Trent & Peak Archaeology during repaving work during which medieval deposits at the west of the Ducal Palace were observed. A stretch of curtain wall, possibly dating to the thirteenth century, was uncovered as was a robber trench where part of the wall had been removed at the west range in the Upper Bailey.[166]

Four very large post holes and two connecting wall trenches were excavated and were thought to be evidence of a substantial timber structure pre-dating the stone wall and may have been remains of the timber watch tower documented as being repaired in 1251.[167]

A twin stairwell or roofed lodge was found, leading from the palace terrace, under the boundary wall to the cliff edge, where it possibly led down to the Park during the mid eighteenth century, providing a quick way for the Duke to access what was the more scenic part of the town.[168]

A watching brief was undertaken during the rebuilding of the outer wall of the Castle's Upper Bailey, once again by Trent & Peak Archaeology, following its collapse in 1996.[169]

On top of the Castle Rock, rock cut pits or post holes were excavated and may form evidence of timber structures of the early timber castle. A small amount of evidence for sandstone building was tied into this phase.[170]

A wall was found cutting through deposits dated to between 1140 and 1180 possibly forming evidence of improvements to the castle known to have occurred in the 1170s. Evidence of further wall building was found, probably dating to the renovations of the Upper Bailey buildings in 1358–67. Evidence of the destruction of the medieval castle and landscaping for the Ducal Palace was also found.[171]

In the 1930s Campion believed he found evidence for a timber structure which stood against the base of the Castle Rock, the land around which he believed had been raised approximately 12ft (3.7m) to raise it above flood level. The evidence for this alleged structure is the weather worn holes and niches in the rock but this is far from convincing. There is no evidence for his elaborate two storey structure with arrow slits. The considerable raising of the ground level is no doubt true though. It is known, through documentation, that mills and other buildings existed at the foot of the Castle Rock by the Leen. Doubtless the land was raised to prevent flooding of those buildings.[172]

These excavations helped corroborate and complement the documentation. As such we now know much about the castle even if much of it cannot be seen.

We know a castle was first constructed under the order of William Peveril shortly after the conquest and consisted of timber bailey, with earthwork defences exploiting the natural sandstone outcrop.

During the twelfth century the castle began to be rebuilt in stone. The Outer Bailey defences were established to divide an outer enclosure into northern and southern areas during the eleventh century whilst the castle was timber and would have joined the post-Conquest defensive ditch and bank at Posterngate. Originally the defences consisted of a ditch, earth rampart and timber palisade, with the palisade being replaced by a curtain wall during either the reign of Henry III (1216–72) or Edward I (1272–1307). The original timber defences of the Upper Bailey were replaced in 1171–73 by a stone curtain wall, which was increased in height in 1185–87. In 1188 the castle had a stone keep, repaired in that year. A stone tower was built in 1212–13 and a round tower was built in 1243 but some timber structures remained, including a wooden watchtower which was in a state of decay in 1251.[173]

Although development continued throughout the medieval period the castle's basic plan created during the reign of Henry II was retained for the next 500 years. The keep was positioned on the highest ground and was approached by a long ramp and cut off from the inner bailey by a steep cliff and deep dry moat. The inner bailey was on much lower ground and surrounded at the north and east by a deep dry moat. The inner bailey contained the Great Hall, kitchens and chapel. A drawbridge would have connected the castle with the extensive outer bailey. A round tower was constructed at the north east of Richard's Tower in the thirteenth century and is known as the Black Tower. The semi circular towers and gatehouse were later additions, probably in the fourteenth century. From the fourteenth century onwards the walls of the outer bailey were joined to the town wall. In 1476 Edward IV ordered the construction of a new tower and Royal Apartments which the following century were still regarded as highly impressive, with Leland describing them in 1540 as 'the most beautifulest part and gallant building for lodging... a right sumptus piece of stone work.'[174]

During the reign of Richard III (1483–85) there were further substantial changes with a hexagonal tower (known as Richard's Tower), constructed at the north-west of the Middle Bailey. Richard visited Nottingham Castle frequently and indeed it was from there that he travelled to Bosworth Field for his fateful meeting with Henry Tudor.[175]

Some of the caves cut into the Castle Rock were associated with the medieval castle. The first reference to such a cave is from 1194–95 and relates to a 'postern giving access to the motte' and this is thought to relate to the passage known today as Mortimer's Hole.

Yet once the medieval period had ended kings and queens were unable to maintain any interest in Nottingham and its castle and by 1603 the castle was no longer occupied, had fallen into disrepair and was partly pulled down. In fact it was described by Leland as being partly in ruins when he visited in 1540.

By 1620, the stone from the castle was being robbed and the condition and importance of this structure which had been a key part of William the Conqueror's strategy in England deteriorated. The castle's inclusion in the history books would most likely have ended there if it had not been for the growing hostility between king and country which led to King Charles I raising the Royal Standard nearby in 1643 and in doing so declaring war against his own parliament.

Later captured by the Parliamentarians, the castle formed an important base for their campaign against the Royalists.[176]

After the cessation of hostilities the castle once again fell to disuse and permission was granted for its demolition, which took place in 1651 with the aid of gunpowder. The land passed to the Duke of Newcastle who had been loyal to the cause against the reckless king.

The site lay vacant until 1674 when clearance and landscaping work was undertaken in advance of the construction of the extant Ducal Palace. The Ducal Palace was built on the site of the medieval castle, on the instruction of the Duke of Newcastle (who died before its completion) in 1679. It was restored in the nineteenth century following arson in 1831 carried out by the Chartists, which reduced the building to little more than a shell although many original features of its late seventeenth century construction survive.

The site (with the exception of the footprint of the Ducal Palace) is now a Scheduled Monument protecting everything below ground level including the numerous caves. Although a large amount of the structure was destroyed there is a possibility that structural remains of the medieval castle may survive, particularly in the castle green area where landscaping has led to deep deposits being laid on top of any surviving masonry and features, thus helping to preserve them. Perhaps in the future more of this famous castle will be revealed.

Nottingham City Council plans to create a unique tourist attraction at Nottingham castle, placing emphasis unfortunately on Robin Hood but also trying to reconstruct small parts, where appropriate, of the medieval castle. Any future work at the castle will result in further archaeological investigation which could help develop our knowledge further.

The Defence of the Town

Following the Norman Conquest the new town of Nottingham, as it came to be called, comprising the former Saxon settlement at the east and the castle at the west, lay unprotected save for its natural features. Domesday records that by 1086 even the defences of the pre-Conquest borough had been filled in.

Excavations have, however, revealed evidence for town defences comprising a ditch and a bank which were eventually created at least three or four decades after the conquest (if the professional archaeological dating is correct) and developed during the medieval period. A stone wall was later built around part of the town.

During works on Maid Marian Way between 1963–64 a stretch of a ditch was found which it was determined was the post-Conquest town ditch which had been created to defend the town and mark its extent. A bank was found associated with the ditch, containing pottery thought to date no later than the twelfth century. The base of the ditch could not be fully investigated and the upper fills had been damaged during machining but it was clear it had been cleaned out on a number of occasions during its use, and had probably been filled in during the eighteenth century.[177]

In 1967 and 1968 during the building of the Mount Street Bus Station the ditch was encountered again. There were relatively few finds within the fills and so it was difficult to date when the ditch might have been created or when it fell out of use. It had not been filled by the time of the town wall being robbed and demolished, which it will be shown was largely in the seventeenth century. It had, however, been partly filled before being re-cut to empty and enlarge the ditch.[178]

In 1970, during excavations at Theatre Square to create a subway, a 21ft (6.4m) length of the southern lip of the post Conquest ditch was found along with a bank. The following year the inner lip of the ditch and bank were excavated on the corner of Maid Marian Way and

Chapel Bar in 1971. The ditch extended under the pavement and was believed to be approximately 19ft (5.8m) wide. Some slight evidence for a rampart was found.[179]

The Woolpack Lane excavation revealed the post-Conquest ditch and it was found to partly use the same line of the pre-Conquest ditch. The post-Conquest ditch was dated to no earlier than 1100, with small re-cuts of the ditch having taken place between c. 1150 and c. 1250.[180]

The archaeology at Woolpack Lane suggests that during the late thirteenth century a new ditch was created utilising much of the earlier ditch but widening it in places and extending it a little further east, to enclose a slightly larger area.[181]

We can use this archaeological knowledge to complement historic sources and show the development of Nottingham's defences.

It is thought the original post Conquest ditch was dug in the first

The pre-Conquest (right) and post-Conquest twelfth century ditches (left) as excavated at Woolpack Lane. (Nottingham City Museums and Galleries, NCMG 2013–4)

half of the twelfth century and enclosed both the 'English' and 'French' boroughs (the English Borough being that area of the Lace Market and the small expansion north and westwards as the population increased, with the French Borough being concentrated towards the west of the town close to the castle, named the French Borough after the invading Normans). A document dating to some point between 1250 and 1263 from St John's Hospital located immediately north of the ditch referred to 'the new ditch', suggesting the second ditch enlarging the defences, re-cutting the earlier ditch, was created around the mid thirteenth century.[182]

The Park Row excavations suggest silting of the ditch occurred between the thirteenth and seventeenth centuries on this part of the ditch close to the castle, on the west of the town, suggesting the ditch was functional well into the post-medieval period. The historic maps do not show it, although Badder and Peat's map of 1744 shows Butt Dyke, which was on the projection of the ditch and may have been part of it or merely the name of a road built on top of the filled ditch. It is my personal belief that much of the ditch was filled long before the seventeenth century but that it was re-cut to form a Civil War defensive feature, and then became filled in by the end of the seventeenth century. This will be discussed in a later chapter.

The Town Rental of 1435 shows that by that year sections of the ditch east of Carter Gate and at the bottom of Barker Gate were being let to private persons to accommodate barns and gardens, suggesting the eastern side of the ditch had been filled before this time.[183] If the eastern side of the ditch had been filled in by this date it is quite feasible that the ditch elsewhere was no longer needed.

The town was not only defended by ditches and banks. Today the cities of York and Chester still retain their medieval character in the form of both street patterns and names but also in the form of substantial walls around the town, in particular at York. Nottingham too had a substantial wall around a large proportion of its perimeter, with excavations suggesting it was up to 3m thick.

The wall was built of large blocks of Nottingham Castle Sandstone with ashlar facing. Where bonded, the bonding material was usually the distinctive red coloured Keuper Marl clay and occasionally lime mortar.

During the Second Barons' Wars (1264–67), according to historic documents, the town was sacked and burnt on three occasions, and this may explain why murage grants (a form of tax) began to be levied occasionally between 1267 and 1337 to fund the construction of a stone wall. Construction may have commenced prior to, and extended beyond, these years, however.

Excavations and observations have shown the wall extended from the curtain wall of the castle and was present at Cumberland Place, running parallel with but east of Park Row, 1–5 Maid Marian Way, Chapel Bar, and along Upper Parliament Street and Lower Parliament Street. The wall is believed to have run around only part of the medieval town. It appears the wall was never completed. There is no evidence of it having extended eastwards beyond Clinton Street.

Documentary evidence also suggests the wall did not extend around the whole town. Why it was not completed is not known. Perhaps it was too big a project, with limited resources, or it was simply believed to be unnecessary to complete it. Indeed by 1395 parts of the wall were already being robbed, with four men standing before the Mickleton Jury in that year charged with the offence of taking away parts of the masonry. In 1408 a hole had been knocked through the wall and in 1538, when Leland visited Nottingham, he recorded that 'much of the Waul is now down' and the gates saving 2 or 3. There were 6 or 7 gates in the Towne waulle. Now all be downe save 3.'[184] Clearly at least some of the town's people did not feel it had any security benefits for them by the late fourteenth century and saw it as a source of free building materials instead.

By 1610 the only stretch of wall surviving was from Chapel Bar to Postern Street, if Speede's map of that year is to be believed, and the archaeology shows that even much of that stretch had been partially demolished by then.

Nonetheless archaeology and antiquarian observations, particularly during the Victorian period, have given us a good understanding of the wall's nature and extent.

According to the Reverend Orange, who lived during the early nineteenth century, traces of the wall were discovered by workmen digging the foundations of the Shakespeare Inn at Ropers Close, which was just north east of Chapel Bar. It was also discovered at Milton Street. He also noted the existence of the wall in the foundations of the houses in the middle of Parliament Row, which was known as Bunker's Hill.[185] Deering had noted the existence of the wall at Bunker's Hill a century earlier, describing it as 'plainly discernable it serving for a foundation to many houses.'[186] It comes as little surprise, therefore, that when the houses were demolished in 1884, part of the wall was encountered.

In 1866 during sewerage works a section of the wall was exposed and photographed at the top of Market Street, in front of the statue of Queen Victoria which once stood there.[187]

In 1897 during the excavation of the railway cutting at Parliament Street, approximately 36 yards (32.9m) of the town wall was seen by Shipman, at a depth of between 21ft and 23ft (6.4–7.0m) below Parliament Street, with a semi-circular buttress having been present. At one point it survived at a depth of only 18 inches (46cm) below street level, where disturbance had until then been minimal. At this point an 'ancient passage' was cut into the wall and led down to a flight of steps in a westerly direction into a later cave.[188]

Stapleton also observed part of the wall during work in advance of the cutting, close to the junction of Parliament Street and Clinton Street but he 'mislaid' his notes.[189]

In 1898 a section of the wall and part of a buttress were observed during the excavations for an underground toilets between the upper ends of Market Street and Queen Street. The stone was composed of blocks of sandstone bound with red clay and it had been robbed of its facing stones.[190]

In January 1898 Shipman observed a wall at the corner of Heathcoat Street and Cranbrook Street during the digging of foundations for a warehouse. At first it was believed the wall was part of the town wall but Shipman later believed this was not the case.[191]

A section of town wall found during the creation of the Great Central Railway. Reproduced from Shipman, 1899.

In 1899 a square buttress and section of town wall were found during excavations opposite South Sherwood Street.[192]

In 1908 back near the statue of Queen Victoria at the top of Market Street more of the wall was found during the laying of water pipes. A further stretch was exposed on Parliament Street at around the same time whilst electricity cables were being laid.[193]

In 1929 following the demolition of the Three Crowns public house at the junction of Parliament Street, Market Street and Theatre Square,

A drawing by Clements of the town wall as discovered in the cellar during the demolition of the Three Crowns on Parliament Street in 1929. (Courtesy of Nottingham City Council and www.picturethepast.co.uk)

during the widening of the road, a section of the town wall was found in the cellar and was drawn by Clements.

When the Cripples' Guild (17–19 Park Row) was being built in 1925, a stretch of the town wall was exposed, running parallel with the road but set back approximately 10m from it. It was clear that at some point in history stone from the wall had been robbed, but it was unclear when this had taken place. The wall was obviously very visually impressive to those who saw it in 1925 because a small length of it was taken down and carefully rebuilt in the garden at 15 Park Valley.[194] A further stretch was found on the west of the building in 1938.[195]

The Corporation of Nottingham discovered a small portion of the medieval town wall whilst demolishing properties between Park Row and Chapel Bar in 1958 to make way for Maid Marian Way. The wall was wider here than in some other locations such as at the end of Market Street and its appearance was different to where it had been encountered elsewhere. The differences in style and construction led the eminent archaeologist Maurice Barley to suggest that this stretch of wall was actually constructed during the twelfth century, long before the 1267 murage grants began to be levied.[196] It is possible some of the town was defended with a wall at this time but it seems unlikely that

The medieval town wall as excavated in 1958. With the 1950s formal attire and numerous health and safety issues, it is a far cry from modern day archaeological practice. (Courtesy of the Nottingham Evening Post and www.picturethepast.co.uk)

even a short stretch of the town defences would have consisted of stone at a time when those closest to the castle, and indeed the castle itself, were built of earth and timber. With the greatest respect to an important figure in archaeology, I have little doubt Barley was incorrect.

A substantial length of the town wall covering more than 30m, was discovered during works to extend Maid Marian Way in 1963–64. The wall was found to be 7ft 3 in (2.2m) thickness except for a length of about 160 ft (48.8m) from Chapel Bar southwards, which was only 5ft (1.5m) thick, and which was on a slightly different alignment to that further north. Effectively there was a kink in the wall as if two stretches of wall had been created starting from different directions and they had failed to meet in the middle. The presence of a clay pipe dating to c. 1630–60 in a robber trench suggested the wall had been robbed at that time.[197]

During the building of the bus station on Mount Street in 1967 and 1968 a number of stretches of the town wall were encountered. Evidence suggested it had been built slowly by different groups of people at different times, which would seem sensible given the earlier discovery of the kink, described above. Again there was evidence that the wall had been partially robbed in the early seventeenth century.[198]

An excavation led by Alan MacCormick and staff from Nottingham City Museums Field Archaeology Section at Theatre Square in 1970 revealed a 22ft (6.7m) stretch of the town wall. It too had been extensively robbed, probably in the late sixteenth century.[199]

The town wall was excavated by the Nottingham Flying Squad at the corner of Maid Marian Way and Chapel Bar in 1971 and was found to have been inserted into the twelfth century bank, as at Theatre Square and elsewhere.[200]

It is unfortunate that so much of the wall has been destroyed. However, a small stretch found under 1–5 Maid Marian Way (currently part of the Holiday Inn Express), is on public display from Maid Marian Way and is protected as a Scheduled Monument. It is approximately 3m in length and 2.2m in width at its base. It has been studied by Trent & Peak Archaeology who found that this portion of the wall was constructed of limestone of at least two phases, showing

One small portion of the medieval town wall can still be seen today and is designated a Scheduled Monument. (The Author)

it had been modified or repaired. Like many walls, this wall was subjected to graffiti both in modern times but also in c. 1760. Post-medieval cellar walls cut the medieval wall suggesting that the graffiti was created by workmen undertaking the construction of a building on top of the wall, rather than that the wall remained visible into the eighteenth century.[201]

The wall is known to have had a number of gates as openings, allowing access and egress to and from the town. Very little archaeological or antiquarian work has been undertaken which has contributed to our knowledge of the gates in the town wall but it is important to briefly describe them in order to have a better understanding of the wall.

The main point of access to the town was the Chapel Bar at the north west of the town defences, where the street named Chapel Bar meets Maid Marian Way today. It is believed the first mention of the gate is that relating to the 'westbarre' (although this may be the name of a gate close to the castle later known as the Postern Gate)[202] and was in use into the eighteenth century when it was demolished in 1743. During the Civil War, new gates or doors were fitted and other improvements and repairs made, but by c. 1700 it was in a ruinous condition.[203] Prior to demolition it consisted of two bastilles each with a large arched roof. On the south side there was an opening under the gate and a guard room. There was a chapel located at the gate, with a door on the north side having led to a room with altars. Towards the end of its life it was used as a brewhouse for the adjacent Fox and Goose Inn.

A drawing of Chapel Bar, the main entrance into Nottingham during the medieval and early post medieval periods. This image shows Chapel Bar in the seventeenth century and is reproduced from Thoroton, 1797.

This image shows Chapel Bar in the eighteenth century shortly before its demolition and is reproduced from Deering, 1740.

A town gate known as St John's Bar, formed an opening in the town wall at the north of the town. Shipman believed this was an alternate name for the Swine Bar, because known historic sources mentioned the St John name only once but perhaps it was an additional gate which was not in use for a lengthy period of time.[204]

A town gate known as Cow Bar or Cow Lane Bar, at the north of the medieval town, was in existence in 1335 and demolished in 1649.[205] This was located where Clumber Street met Parliament Street. In 1811 Stretton observed remains of what he believed was the Cow

Bar during street works at the junction of Clumber Strete and Parliament Street.[206] Three years later a large number of green glazed ecclesiastical style floor tiles were found at Clumber Street, leading Stretton to speculate that the gate may have had an associated chapel.[207]

Swine Bar or Swine Bar Gate, formed an opening at the north east of the medieval town and was so named because it was the gate used by the swineherd which were taken to the town wood each day and brought back to be penned on the Swine Green at night (it being illegal for the owners of pigs to have them on their own property). This gate was first mentioned in 1408.[208]

Shipman speculated that there was an eastern gate to the town. A gate called Carter Gate was recorded in 1583 and although Speede's map labels Carter Gate where Cow Bar is known to have existed, this was probably an error, with Carter Gate existing where the street Carter Gate is located today as it was in medieval times, on the east side of the town.[209] It makes sense that although there was no wall on the east side of the town there was still the need for some form of defences and an access point to Sneinton would have been necessary. Gates did exist after the wall was destroyed showing that they still retained an important function even when there was no wall.

A number of observations by antiquarians such as Deering in the eighteenth century and excavations, particularly by Campion and Wass, identified stretches of walls towards the south of the medieval town which were speculated to form a southern defensive wall. The Reverend Orange described the wall as extending across Fisher Gate to Hollowstone 'where a portion of the wall was lately visible.' He added that the wall was revealed in 1829 when some of the cliff fell at the rear of the Loggerheads and apparently some of the stone was used to pave the rear of the public house which had to be rebuilt because it was damaged by the rock fall. It then ran west down Garners Hill 'where a part of the old wall is distinctly visible above the ground, near to a small shop occupied by Mr John Smith, lace agent.'[210] Deering wrote that in his lifetime the wall was still visible in places on the bottom of Low Pavement despite being built on. Wass believed he had seen the wall on Castle Gate. He also noted the discovery of part of a very strongly bound wall being discovered at Hollowstone.[211]

However, modern archaeologists have argued there is insufficient evidence of a wall having extended along the south of the town, or of any building programme having been planned,[212] although that is not to say individual wealthy landowners did not build small stretches of substantial walls as boundaries or defensive features for their own properties. The problem is that any stretch of wall that was substantial and appeared to be medieval was considered, often without reason, to be part of the town wall. Certainly, however, there were substantial walls to the south of the town. Were they defences? At Fisher Gate a substantial wall was discovered, which would on the face of it appear to have been a defensive feature and could conceivably be part of the same wall seen by Deering. However, it was found to date to the late-medieval period at a time when the defences elsewhere in the town were becoming redundant.[213]

Whilst southern defences may not have consisted of a wall, at least of the same nature as that at the north, with the cliff line still forming a natural defence, the south certainly had a guarded entrance at the top of Drury Hill.

In 1875 during alterations to a public house, which was then known as the Postern Gate Inn, but which had originally been the Bull's Head, substantial medieval masonry was encountered. Rough drawings and measurements were, however, made by one of the contractors.[214]

When the Inn was demolished in 1910 excavations by Dobson provided a clearer plan of the structure, which was roughly square shaped in plan, and which it was believed may have been built between 1280 and 1320. On the basis of a description by Deering, quoted below, it was concluded it was destroyed in c. 1735–40 when the Bull's Head was built on its foundations. Enough of the structure survived to establish its plan. The room was found to be facing Bridlesmith Gate with a window on its east side and a second window facing Weekday Cross. Its walls ranged in thickness between approximately 1m and 1.5 m.[215]

It was described by Deering (c. 1745–50) as being a 'gate-house where a guard was kept' and he noted it had been in existence 'within these ten years.'[216] It was also observed by the Reverend Orange and Shipman, who drew the structure.

Dobson's guardhouse, as the structure has become known, does suggest some sort of guarded or defended southern boundary but certainly not as substantial as those around much of the north.

A Town of Two Peoples

Excavations by Campion and the Thoroton Society Excavation Section at the Old Market Square during the Second World War, whilst water tanks were being installed by the Air Raid Precautions personnel, revealed the foundations of a wall and what Campion believed to be a pre existing boundary ditch on the south side of the wall, measuring 8ft (2.4m) in width and 4.5ft (1.4m) in depth. There is no other evidence for the ditch and the excavation was restricted to a small test pit excavation in each corner of the Market Square. As such the extent of the feature he believed to be a ditch could not be established. Sadly few details of the wall are recorded in his excavation summary.[217]

During redevelopment of the Market Square in 2006 a watching brief was undertaken in three areas of the Old Market Square by Gavin Kinsley working for Trent & Peak Archaeology. In one area part of a 5.7m length of a mortared brick wall was found on stone foundations only a small depth below the surface. It was identified as being part of a wall shown on Speede's map of 1610 and Thoroton's map of 1677, and presumably the same wall as seen by Campion more than sixty years earlier. There was no sign of an earlier phase to the wall. The wall had clearly originally been a stone structure with some brick repair, rebuild or modification towards the end of its use. A series of small pits or post holes south of the wall, dating to later than the wall's construction, could have been evidence of a replacement fence or a structure.[218]

This wall was identified correctly by Campion and Kinsley as being the market wall, which divided the Old Market Square running down Long Row and approximately east to west across the Old Market Square. Documentation referred to it being 'breast height', with several openings in it. The earliest reference for the wall dates to 1530 and it is known it required repairing in 1579.[219]

Why was a dividing wall needed? It has been speculated that the wall was in place to separate livestock from produce,[220] but this was a problem common to all markets yet other markets did not have such a feature and the presence of gaps in the wall would render it ineffective for this purpose.

A more likely explanation was put forward by former City Council documentary historian Stefan Mastoris. His belief was that the market wall was formed to mark a boundary between land belonging to two groups of people.[221] A relatively little known fact about Nottingham's past is that following the Norman conquest it consisted of two boroughs known as the French Borough and the English Borough, with each area having distinct laws, punishments, customs and administration, each having its own Moot Hall where justice was served, with the English borough having its Moothall located on Weekday Cross and the French Borough having its Moothall located on Friar Lane. One distinction in terms of the law was that in the French Borough upon the death of the father inheritance passed to the oldest son, whilst in the English Borough inheritance passed to the youngest son. Another distinction was that each borough had its own bailiff, later referred to as a Sheriff. The existence of two sheriffs of Nottingham until the fifteenth century is something which does not feature in any tale of Robin Hood.[222]

Originally the English Borough consisted of the area which had defined the pre-Conquest borough but as the population increased it expanded, as did the French Borough which began close to the castle. However, there were problems caused by the fact that the English Borough had different laws and punishments than those of the French Borough. With half of the market being within the English Borough and half in the French Borough this raised a problem in that if a crime was committed it would be essential to establish which borough the crime was committed in, and no doubt there were financial differences between the two halves of the market.[223]

It is probably no coincidence that when this distinction between an English and French population ended, remarkably only in 1714 when the two authorities were merged to form one council which began to meet in the old Exchange building on the site of the present building in 1724, the market wall was demolished although it was only entirely removed in 1728 when the market square was repaved.

It is true to say that other than the laws and traditions which they followed it does not appear that the occupants of the French Borough lived tremendously differently to those in the English part of the town and it would seem they lived in relative peaceful coexistence, with the differences between them gradually becoming less noticeable until the two populations became one.

Medieval Houses

It has already been said that the Domesday survey of 1086 recorded there were 191 houses in the pre-Conquest borough of Nottingham, 48 of which were merchants houses, and that 23 houses had been built on the filled in pre-Conquest ditch. Thanks to Robin Hood movies and other depictions of medieval England in television and film, the general public could be forgiven for thinking that the majority of people in this country lived in little more than mud huts or ramshackle sheds during the medieval period. Thankfully archaeology has offered some information as to what houses and other buildings may have looked like during the medieval period. It has also provided some evidence for when parts of Nottingham were occupied.

We know from documentary sources that during the reign of King Stephen (1135–54) there were two tremendous fires in Nottingham. The first was in 1140 when the town was set alight under the orders of the Empress Matilda and a number of residents of the St Peter's parish were massacred in the church as they hid. The second fire was in 1153.[224] Although there is no direct archaeological evidence for this, there is some evidence of boundaries changing during the mid twelfth century, as if houses were demolished, sites reorganised and new buildings built.

Archaeology has shown that most houses would have been made of timber, with stone becoming increasingly used as the medieval period progressed but only for those with a degree of wealth.

During the Drury Hill excavation a probable eleventh century substantial timber enclosure fence was found built into the filled pre-Conquest ditch. The fence consisted of two lines of stake holes running east to west across the ditch. It showed that soon after the conquest the ditch was filled and occupation quickly spread onto it. A number of timber structures were also found on the filled in ditch at Drury Hill. One of the buildings was timber framed and could be dated by pottery and a silver halfpenny to the reign of Henry I (1100–35). The occupation of the site continued, with timber buildings being found dating from the twelfth to fourteenth centuries.[225]

During archaeological investigations at nearby Garner's Hill evidence for possible timber buildings was found to date to the early post-Conquest period, at a time when exposed bedrock formed the ground surface. During the mid- to late-medieval period stone buildings were present at the southern end of the site.[226]

There is some evidence of highly significant medieval buildings in the Lace Market. Post holes representing a 60ft (18.3m) long building were found on Drury Hill, which was believed to date to the mid thirteenth century. Beneath the buildings, and associated with it, was a rock cut undercroft which was older than the building suggesting it had belonged to a previous building but was reused by the substantial building. What was the function of the building? Its size alone suggests it was high status.[227]

The excavation at Halifax Place also revealed important buildings showing the site's significance continued beyond the Saxon period. Unusually, at a time when buildings were built of timber, on this site there was a stone building erected between c. 1070 to 1140. Could it have been associated with the immediate aftermath of the Norman Conquest? Could it even have been used as a mint? Its location in the English Borough would suggest not but it seems most likely that the minting of coins continued where it had during Saxon times and so there is the likelihood that the Normans had some activities within the former pre-Conquest borough. It was certainly an important building or had a function which required it to be built in stone at a time when even the castle was only constructed of timber. The stone building was destroyed or damaged by fire and two timber buildings constructed in its place in c. 1140. A small bronze staff head, roughly the size of a ping pong ball, was found on the site. Although a very small number of staff heads of similar appearance have been found, the one discovered at Halifax Place is of a different style. It is considered to reflect high status, perhaps ceremonial activity.[228]

The site continued to be systematically developed and redeveloped until c. 1350 when the site became a garden and remained so until the eighteenth century.[229]

The Fisher Gate excavations revealed a series of timber buildings constructed between the eleventh and thirteenth centuries. A half timber/half stone building and three large timber buildings were demolished c. 1350 and the site was then abandoned.[230]

The Goose Gate excavations revealed evidence of occupation from the twelfth century onwards, with evidence of timber buildings dating to c. 1125–c.1250 fronting Goose Gate.[231]

The Boots Garage excavations revealed a sequence timber buildings was revealed on the frontage of Woolpack Lane between the eleventh century and the late thirteenth century, A mid-thirteenth century rock-cut undercroft with stepped entrance, timber framed doorway and settings for structural features was found which were associated with timber outbuildings. Very little activity took place on the site between the fourteenth and seventeenth centuries and it is possible the site was abandoned for much of this period.[232]

Clearly much of the area of the Lace Market was abandoned during the fourteenth century. The reason is uncertain. Around this time, in 1349, a substantial amount of England's population was wiped out by the Black Death but there is no known documentation indicating any impact of the disease, or any significant loss of life, in Nottingham. That is not to say the plague did not hit Nottingham. It would seem that it probably did hit Nottingham and that there is just a lack of documentation. Certainly the abandonment of part of the town would suggest a sudden reduction in population. In 1376 houses were noted as being in a state of severe dereliction.[233] Whatever had happened in the mid fourteenth century, there was no quick recovery and indeed things would get much worse when in 1433–34 a Royal Charter remarked upon Nottingham being an impoverished town.[234] A century later in 1535–36), according to Deering, there was a Royal Order from Henry VIII for the 're-edifying' of Nottingham, Gloucester , Northampton , and other towns. According to Deering the text stated that there were many houses in Nottingham and the other towns which were in 'great ruin and decay' and that there were 'pyttes, cellars and vaults, lying open and uncovered, very perillous for people to go by in the Nyghte withoute Jeopardy of Lyf.'[235] Even the maps of Speede and Thoroton show the area was still largely abandoned centuries later.

In a few instances actual upstanding structural remains have survived from the medieval period, offering a real insight into their appearance.

The most notable of these is the Severns building which, until recently was the Nottingham Lace Centre. It is currently located on Castle Road but was originally situated on Middle Pavement. When the Broadmarsh Shopping Centre was built this historic building had

An extract of Thoroton's map of Nottingham dating to 1677, which shows that the land to the east of St Mary's church was still largely abandoned in the seventeenth century. Archaeology suggests the abandonment took place three centuries earlier.

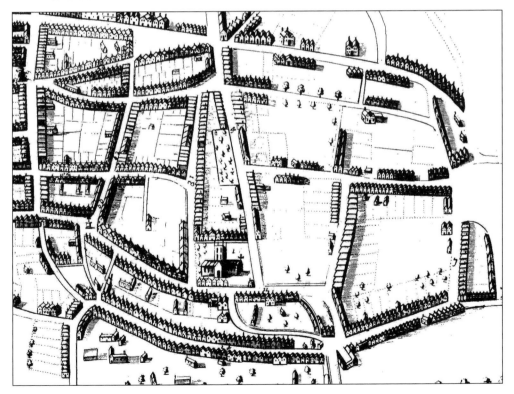

not been considered, largely because it was not understood to be medieval at that time, and so its destruction was ordered. The plans for the centre could not be changed but a campaign resulted in a full survey of the building, followed by its careful demolition. It was then rebuilt in 1970 on its current site and restored to its original appearance without the plaster which had coated its frontage during its recent history on the Middle Pavement site.[236]

Many original architectural features were found to have survived, including a rafter roof and timber frame which were thought to date the building to c. 1450. A timber framed floor and four large bridging

This timber framed building once stood on Middle Pavement and was due to be destroyed when the Broadmarsh Centre was built. Following a successful campaign it was carefully demolished and rebuilt on Castle Road. It dates to the medieval period. (The Author)

beams enabled the building to be supported whilst spanning a cave under the building whilst at Middle Pavement. It has been empty and up for sale for some time and we can only hope it is bought soon and by some individual or organisation that will ensure its future is protected. The importance of the building cannot be underestimated. Although it has been taken apart and rebuilt it remains quite possibly Nottingham's oldest building.[237] Although the style is suggestive of the mid fifteenth century, dendrochronology of timbers has suggested elements of the building actually date to a century earlier. One sample of timber was dated to c. 1338 give or take five years, a second sample dated to timber felled at some time between 1335 and 1353 and a third sample being found to be reused timber which could have dated as early as 1130.[238]

The Bell Inn public house on Angel Row was first mentioned in 1638 in the will of Robert Sherwin, and described as being a 'Messuage or Tenement called by the name of the Bell', although the structure of much of the present building is more recent. However, parts of the building date from the medieval period.[239] Dendrochronology of the remains of the crown-post roof gave an estimate of 1432–52 with the 1430s being the most likely date, though that only dates the timber, it does not necessarily mean the roof was built at that time but it is certain the roof, and therefore the building as a whole, was built in the mid fifteenth century, with later changes being made.[240]

The building which stands at 11 Bridlesmith Gate is four storeys high with a jettied attic. Modifications were made during the eighteenth and nineteenth century and more recently, with a modern shop frontage. This has disguised its much earlier origins; dendrochronology and a building survey have shown it to have been a timber framed house constructed in the fifteenth century. Timbers have been dated to 1443.[241]

The building at 54–56 Bridlesmith Gate has original possible late-medieval features including timber beams in the ground floor area. The original timber frame structure is of a style dating to c. 1550 although it has been suggested it is no earlier than 1600.[242] It is possible the building may be very early post-medieval but its survival is remarkable nonetheless and the building would still have some features in common with medieval buildings of that area.

Fragments of medieval buildings have been found during demolition of buildings whose antiquity had not been recognised until the demolition crews moved in. Examples of this were a fragment of medieval timber-framed building standing against 19 Bridlesmith Gate,[243] a probable medieval timber framed wall in the side of a building on or adjacent to 26–28 Bridlesmith Gate[244] and timbers at The Windmill public house on Weekday Cross. During demolition of the pub possible medieval timbers were seen, although they were described at the time as being possibly late sixteenth century.[245]

Although a large part of the Lace Market was abandoned in the fourteenth century, and the economic wellbeing of the town declined by the 1430s, as the seventeenth century commenced expansion began in earnest. Speede's map of 1610 shows two rows of dwellings north of the line of the town wall, which had largely been destroyed by that time.[246] Pottery production had long taken place beyond the town wall, but there had been no evidence of permanent habitation north of the defences until this time. Subsequent historic maps show this trend of expansion beyond the limits of the defences had continued. Archaeology has shown caves outside the town defences dating to this period, with post-medieval caves as cellars up Mansfield Road in particular. Nottingham was expanding from its own constraints of the medieval town.

Churches, Chapels, Friaries and Hospitals

A number of religious institutions are referred to in documentation about Nottingham's past but usually there is no archaeological evidence relating to them on account of development having destroyed any evidence or the site of the institution being unknown. For example, St Mary's Lazar hospital for Lepers is known to have been located near Chapel Bar, outside the town defences, and was referred to in 1330[247] but there is no archaeology for it. The same is true of St Leonards Hospital which was also established for the care and confinement of sufferers of this terrible affliction. Only those in existence during medieval times, where archaeology has assisted in our understanding will be discussed here, but archaeology has been undertaken for all of the key institutions.

It should be emphasised here that the word hospital in the context of a medieval institution is not the same as the modern understanding of the word. Hospitals in medieval times were generally buildings established for the benefit of the poor and needy, not necessarily just the ill, and religion played a major role in their administration and day to day running. They were usually owned, or at least financed, by a church and usually contained a chapel for worship of the divine but also any earthly benefactors.

The three churches in the medieval town of Nottingham still survive today, as St Mary's, St Peter's and St Nicholas' churches. Archaeology has provided evidence for the history of each of these churches as well as other religious institutions long gone.

Domesday mentioned the existence of one church, which has been presumed to be St Mary's Church on High Pavement, being the only church known in the Lace Market during the medieval period and being within the confines of the pre-Conquest borough standing on the highest point of its land. Thus the site of St Mary's is the most likely location for this early church. There is no evidence within the fabric of the building for St Mary's church during the Saxon period or early post-Conquest period. It is likely later rebuilds and modifications have destroyed, or at least concealed, the earliest remains of the church.

The church today stands as a cruciform building with tower. It has been commonly believed that construction work commenced c. 1376 with later additions, such as the tower being built during the reign of Henry VII (1485 to 1509).[248]

Although extensively modified over the centuries, it is believed that St Mary's is the oldest church in Nottingham and was mentioned in the Domesday Survey of 1086. (The Author)

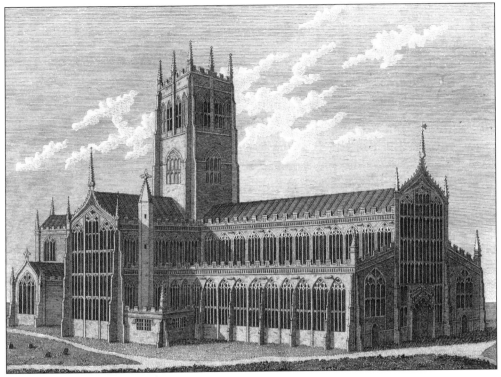

St Mary's Church in the 17th century. Reproduced from Thoroton, 1797.

Indeed Leland described the church as being 'newe and uniform in worke' when he visited the church in c. 1540 but by 1625 it was in need of repair, with further repairs and modifications from the seventeenth to twentieth centuries, changing its character, but it still retains some medieval appearance.[249]

In December 1842 concerns about the safety of the structure led to the foundations of the church being investigated. It was discovered that graves had been dug close to the foundations, partially undermining the structure. Floor tiles and capitals believed to date to the 'late Saxon or early Norman' period, dating to an earlier church on the site, were encountered. These had been reused to form the foundations of the rebuilt church.[250]

St Peter's Church. A church has been present on the site of the current church since the twelfth century. The extant structure mainly dates to the 14th and 15th centuries, with more recent substantial renovations. (The Author)

St Peter's Church in the 17th century. reproduced from Thoroton, 1797

Towards the beginning of the nineteenth century a cave was investigated in the church graveyard, which was accessed by a small trap door. The cave was a 'bone hole' containing a large number of human bones. It is no longer accessible, having been filled in 1912.[251]

St Peter's Church, located on St Peter's Gate, is a church with tower and spire dating to the medieval period. The current church is a rebuild of an earlier church founded in the early twelfth century (William Peveril granted land for the building of the church between 1103 and 1108 and it is likely work commenced soon after). Part of the southern portion of the building has been thought to date to c. 1180, constituting a rebuild following the fire described earlier during the reign of King Stephen, but the style of the building appears to be of a later date.

Certainly a church existed in Norman times but there is no visible trace of it. It is quite possible the earliest architecture visible today dates to the thirteenth century but the majority of it dates to the fourteenth and fifteenth centuries with substantial restorations in the eighteenth, nineteenth and twentieth centuries.[252]

Around 1739 Deering was present in the church whilst the Smith family vault was being made. During the work an arch was found in the north wall below floor level. Within the arch was a stone coffin containing the remains of a body of a man, believed to be John de Plumptre, and a red glazed tile with cross keys on it; a commonly found symbol relating to St Peter.[253]

In 1886 during restoration work, involving the underpinning of the south aisle, remains of a wooden screen were found, possibly dating to the late fourteenth or early fifteenth century. No earlier structural features were observed.[254]

In 1884 during widening of St Peter's Gate, allegedly two thousand burials were exhumed and re-interred elsewhere. However, some burials were encountered at a depth of 17ft (5.2m) and these were not disturbed. They probably still survive under St Peter's Gate and are part of its medieval burial ground.[255]

St Nicholas's Church stands today as a red brick building yet its history has been shown to exist possibly as far back as the eleventh century, shortly after the conquest.

Modifications to the church consisting of foundation trenches for a boiler house and a new church floor at a lower level required watching briefs and an excavation between 1989 and 1991 by Nottingham City Museum Field Archaeology Section. This archaeological work showed the original church was possibly cruciform with a central tower, but the excavation did not go to a sufficient depth to reveal an accurate ground plan. It was suggested the remains of the church, consisting of stone rubble and painted wall plaster, dated to the late eleventh century or possibly earlier; the remains could not be closely dated. The church must have been constructed after 1066, however, to serve the followers of William the Conqueror who inhabited the area close to the castle.[256]

The present St Nicholas Church built in the eighteenth century. (The Author)

In c. 1800 the sexton of the church found masonry believed to be part of the medieval church, whilst digging at the top of Rosemary Lane, a lane which no longer exists. [257] As a result it was wrongly assumed, for the best part of two centuries, that the medieval church had been further north than where the church currently stands.[258] The excavation of 1991 showed the church had been rebuilt on the same spot.

Documentation shows that the church was destroyed during the Civil War in 1643. During the hostilities its tower had been used by the Royalists as a suitable platform to bombard the castle. It was destroyed by the Parliamentarians to prevent a repeated effort. The site remained empty until work began on a rebuild of the church.[259]

A drawing of the previous St Nicholas' Church, which was built and demolished in the late seventeenth century, reproduced from Thoroton, 1797.

Prior to the archaeological work it was believed that no church had existed between 1643 and the building of the red brick church which stands today. Archaeology supported documentation which had always been questioned, showing that another church had existed before the current church was built but that it had only survived a few decades.

The work suggested the short lived stone rebuild of the church was cruciform in plan with a central tower and the stone was ashlar faced. The church was built on substantial stone foundations of the medieval church. A series of plaster floors of the seventeenth century church were discovered. Close dating evidence for this phase of the site's occupation was lacking but timber was ordered for part of the church (possibly the roof) in September 1671 and a drawing of 1680 shows the church with a damaged tower, so it is certain the church was built in the 1670s.[260] Why the tower was in such a poor state so soon after its construction is unknown. Perhaps it was struck by lightening, was vandalised or was built by the seventeenth century equivalent of a cowboy builder.

In c. 1700 the current red brick cruciform structure was built on the same spot as its predecessors, but on a slightly different alignment. It was extended in the eighteenth and nineteenth centuries. Twenty-six burial vaults predating the Victorian era were uncovered and recorded by the archaeologists during the modifications. They were filled with sand to protect them from being disturbed by development. Sadly burials at the church were disturbed in the 1950s when Maid Marian Way was created; the graveyard was reduced in size to make way for the road and a large number of skeletons removed. A cave containing lots of human bones was also encountered. Whilst making Maid Marian Way a Quaker burial ground was also destroyed, with burials from that site also being moved.

Part of the Robin Hood legend sees the involvement of Friar Tuck. Certainly Nottingham had two friaries during the medieval period and archaeological work has furthered our knowledge of them.

While carrying out extensive alterations at the rear of the White Swan Inn on Beastmarket Hill in 1872, seven human skeletons were found at a depth of 5ft to 7ft (1.5m–2.1m).[261]

Just over half a century later, in 1923, whilst renovation work was being undertaken at the Swan Inn, it was necessary to reduce the ground by 11ft (3.4m). The ground reduction revealed a section of boundary wall, and remains of stone buildings near the corner of Friar Lane and Beastmarket Hill. Two human skeletons were found between the buildings. Glazed monastic floor tiles, worked stone and a stone roofing tile were also recovered.[262]

In 1762 labourers discovered a 'great quantity' of human bones amongst which was a reasonably well preserved skeleton of a tall man in a decayed coffin, while digging foundations for a building on

The partial remains of the Carmelite Friary as photographed in the 1920s. (Courtesy of the Thoroton Society of Nottinghamshire and www.picturethepast.co.uk)

Beastmarket Hill. Well preserved door and window fragments and 'curious relics' were also found. Sadly there are no records of these relics.[263]

In 1844 during alterations to a house on Beastmarket Hill, labourers found several human skeletons. One of these was a well preserved skeleton of a tall adult male.[264]

At some time in the mid to late nineteenth century several skeletons and coffins were found during work on Market Place. At least one of the skeletons was preserved so well it still had hair on the head and possibly the tongue and the roof or palate were still preserved.[265]

In 1886 and 1887 human bones were found at the rear of a property close to the junction of Beastmarket Hill and Friar Lane.[266]

Following the work at the White Swan Inn further developments revealed even more burials and remnants of the friary buildings.

In 1947 four skeletons were uncovered during the digging of new foundations for the Friends Meeting House on Friar Lane. Curiously one of the skeletons had mercury in the pelvic recess. My research suggests this could possibly have been because the man whose remains were found had been suffering from syphilis. Mercury was believed to be a possible cure for the disease. If I am correct this would date the skeleton to the later medieval period.[267]

During work to extend a bank on Beastmarket Hill in 1965, wall foundations, presumably of buildings of the friary, and approximately thirteen human burials, with iron nails and coffin clamps, were seen but destroyed without being fully recorded.[268]

These discoveries relate to a friary and its associated burial ground which were known to have existed on the site and which belonged to the Carmelite Friars (also known as the White Friars).

The Carmelite Friary were founded by Reginald Lord Grey de Wilton and Sir John Shirley c. 1276 on land between Friar Lane and St James's Street although there is some evidence that the Friary was operational in 1272 when a grant of oak trees was given.[269] Some religious institutions are known to have existed before they were legally recognised. The friary had a chapel dedicated to St James and its cemetery extended from Friar Lane to St James's Street.

Following the Dissolution it was briefly left abandoned until the estate passed to the Duke of Rutland. The structures in existence when the Duke took over the land were 'a messuage, a swinestye, houses, yards, stables west of the messuage'. There was a garden to the north and an orchard and three acres of pasture land within the boundary walls.[270]

During the construction of a building known as Grosvenor House, on the south side of Friar Lane, in 1938 four caves were encountered, one of which was thought to be a crypt and contained human bones, with evidence of a heavy door having existed to possibly seal the chamber. A cross was carved into the rock above the door to the crypt cave, which was believed to be medieval.[271]

Despite being on the south side of Friar Lane, outside the boundary of the Carmelite Friary, Campion, who visited the caves, believed it might possibly have been associated with the friary but there is no other evidence for this.

In 1937 several stretches of what was believed to be the same wall were found at Grey Friar's Hall, Gordon House, Widdowson's West Wing and Widdowson's East Wing. Campion believed the wall was the boundary wall of a different friary, belonging to the Grey Friars.[272]

In 1775 excavators working on the south side of Broad Marsh discovered a quantity of human bones and skulls, some of which had teeth in perfect condition, thought to be medieval. Within the period 1866–81 (and presumably towards the beginning of that time), during repairs to Carrington Street some human bones were excavated. It is probable both of these discoveries related to the burial ground of the Grey Friar's friary.[273]

Two burial grounds were found at Broad Marsh on the site of a building which belonged to St Peter's Church and were investigated by the Thoroton Society Excavation Section. The highest level contained burials of St Peter's Church, which Campion believed dated to c. 1750 but this must be wrong because the burial ground only opened in 1831. At a lower level were burials which Campion believed dated to c. 1400 and were associated with the Grey Friars burial ground.[274]

The friary of the Franciscans (Grey Friars) was officially founded by Henry III in 1250, but there is some evidence for an earlier foundation, perhaps between 1224 and 1230. The Close Rolls record that on 5 March 1230 the 'Friars Minor of Nottingham' were granted timber for the fabric of their chapel.[275] It was located on the site of where the western half of the Broadmarsh Shopping Centre now stands, with its boundary wall extending as far south as the River Leen.[276] It had the right of burial but only four people are recorded as having been buried in the church, although the archaeology shows a higher number of burials occurred.[277]

By the time of the dissolution the friary had a prior and seven friars. After the dissolution the land and its buildings were used as a lead works.[278]

The hospital of St John the Baptist (also known as Spital House) was a monastic hospital located north of the town defences on the site of what would later become the prison, police and fire station (now close to the junction of King Edward Street and Lower Parliament Street). It has been said to have been founded in King John's reign, and the earliest known reference dates to 1208 when it was considered to have sufficient wealth to be responsible for the upkeep of the Leen bridge.[279]

A request for the right of burial was made in 1220 and certainly burials were taking place on its land by 1234.[280]

It is unknown how many burials took place on the hospital grounds, but only one skeleton has ever been found; that of an adult with a ring on its thumb (it was a custom of the fifteenth and sixteenth centuries to wear a wedding ring on the thumb) during construction of the Nottingham prison during or before 1829.[281]

Where are the other burials? The site was not extensively developed until the nineteenth century and so one would expect burials to have been recorded outside the town defences in this area.

The land was granted to the town at the Dissolution in 1539 to provide funds for the maintenance of the Trent Bridge. By c. 1540 when Leland visited Nottingham he found the building was 'almoste downe'[282] although some of the structures were used for the House of Corrections which was founded in 1611.

I said in an earlier chapter that the Trent Bridge contained a chapel, and other chapels existed at or close to entrances to the town, but archaeological evidence is lacking for most of these. That at the Trent Bridge was dedicated to St James and is mentioned in documentation but little is known about it. Permission was granted for a chapel and two chaplains in 1302 but it was not finished until twenty years later.[283] The chapel appears to have been built on the bridge itself, on the sixth arch. It is thought to have been destroyed during the floods of 1683[284] but Leland failed to mention any chapel in his description of the bridge

A medieval chapel on a bridge in Rotherham. A similar type of chapel existed on the Trent Bridge during the medieval period. (The Author)

in c. 1540 suggesting it had been demolished by then, perhaps at the time of the dissolution.[285] During the nineteenth century evidence for the chapel was found.

Antiquarians have, however, obtained some valuable knowledge of the chapel. During the summer of 1817 a large amount of Gothic stone work was seen on the river bed whilst repairs were being made to the foundations of the Trent Bridge.[286] In July 1826 there was a drought in Nottingham, which resulted in the river level dramatically dropping. This occurrence was used as an opportunity to investigate the condition of the bridge's foundations and whilst the foundations were being examined a large amount of sculptured stone and mullioned windows, resembling those at St Mary's Church, were observed.[287] In 1831 parts of a window, a padlock and chain were found in the river beneath the bridge.[288]

Nottingham was not only home to practicing Christians during medieval times, however. There was a Jewish synagogue as early as 1257, which had a rock cut cellar beneath it. In 1391 the synagogue, known as *Schola Judaeorum* became the home of Henry Plumptre. The street known as St Nicholas Street was once called Jew Lane.[289]

With religion playing a major role in the lives of Nottingham folk during the medieval period it is of great value that archaeology has revealed more about the place where the religion was practiced.

Whiston

Between December 1840 and February 1841 during the construction of a workhouse at York Street, immediately north of where the Victoria Shopping Centre now stands, labourers found part of a tiled pavement, masonry and, more interestingly, a large number of well preserved human bones, a stone coffin and a number of brass rings and brooches. One of the brooches was believed to date to between the thirteenth and fifteenth centuries, but no other details are recorded regarding any of the other artefacts recovered.[290]

The antiquarians of the day believed the discoveries were associated with a church and associated burial ground. Such a church was known from historic texts to have existed outside the town defences during the medieval period in a place known as Whiston which is believed to have been located between Huntingdon Street and York Street. Historic sources suggest St Michael's, as the church was named, was demolished in 1328, and legend states this was the result of violence between soldiers garrisoned in Whiston, though there is little evidence of any disorder and it is unclear where this legend originated. Nonetheless in 1341–42 records stated that St Michael's had only recently been destroyed and the earliest records of the church, which we know about, date to after the church ceased to exist.[291]

Whiston had existed since at least 1217, when the earliest reference to the area was made, and it appears the name continued beyond the demolition of the church, as late as 1514–15 when a license was granted to Hugh de Bell to cultivate land at Wystendale. Whetston Hill mentioned in 1608–09 may also be named after the long gone area.[292]

It is quite puzzling that there was occupation outside the medieval defences at a time when those defences may still have been under construction, certainly if Stevenson and Stapleton are to be believed in their view that St Michael's was 'certainly in existence as early as 1262,'[293] though how they came to this conclusion is unknown. We have already seen that Whiston existed before that time. Certainly it existed in the early fourteenth century. St John's hospital, of course, existed immediately outside the defences, and Lenton Priory and Lenton Hermitage existed to the west of the town but these were religious sites which have been well recorded. There are no records for St Michael's Church contemporary to when activity was taking place there.

In fact could it be coincidence that the town wall ends around Clinton Street, immediately south of where Whiston was supposed to have existed (albeit slightly further east than the western limit of where burials were found associated with St Michael's)? The post-Conquest defensive ditch may have been created along the entirety of the northern limit of the medieval town as it stood in the eleventh and twelfth century but if Whiston came into existence between that time and the time of the construction of the wall (or at least during the sixty or more years during which murage grants for the wall were being levied to raise funds for the ongoing wall building programme) it would have been unnecessary to extend the wall dividing the medieval town from what conceivably could be considered to be a suburb. If I am correct it would appear Whiston became an extended part of the medieval town for the short duration of its existence and that it was founded after the time the latest post-Conquest town ditch was created in the late thirteenth century, but it is still puzzling that it is not referred to in the documentation for the administration of the town, such as the Borough Records. Perhaps the church's documentation was destroyed when the church was destroyed, but it is still remarkable that something so close to the medieval town received so little mention.

Further existence of Whiston was uncovered throughout much of the second half of the nineteenth century. In c. 1860 Shipman saw human bones being found on the corner of Woodborough Road and Mansfield Road, during the widening and lowering of the road surface.[294]

In September 1878, back at the workhouse, more human bones believed to be of approximately twelve individuals were found, with well preserved skulls. A further twenty or more skeletons were found during levelling of a yard at the rear of the workhouse.[295]

Almost twenty years later, in July 1897, in advance of the creation of the Great Central Railway cutting seven or eight more skeletons were found at the north east corner of the site of the workhouse which was demolished at that time. Further remains were found further south, consisting of disarticulated remains and at least thirteen skulls. There was no evidence of coffins or graves and it was Shipman's opinion that the bones had been moved from elsewhere, even if only a short distance. Pottery described as being 'ancient' (the term ancient was misused by antiquarians, with even late-medieval artefacts being described as being ancient) was found but no floor tiles or masonry was encountered. Shipman visited the site several times but saw no evidence for the church or chapel itself.[296]

A century earlier, in April 1796, labourers digging on Woodborough Road (known as Fox Lane at the time) found six complete human skeletons lying side by side. The bones had been damaged, as if the individuals had been in conflict (the labourers imagined). It was a belief of the time, or at least during the Victorian period, that they were victims of Robin Hood and his Merry Men. Though they were also described as being Saxon and had been buried with 'old' coins the likelihood is, given their location, that they were associated with St Michael's and therefore Whiston. The skeletons were reburied on the same site and it is not impossible they were amongst the remains discovered when Woodborough Road was widened and lowered during Victorian times.[297]

Whiston remains somewhat of an enigma. Was it a suburb of the main town of Nottingham or could it have been entirely independent and self governing? There is no known documentation relating to its people paying any levies, fines or other payments to the town. Indeed there is no reference to any named individual. This begs the question of whether Whiston actually had a permanent population or whether it may predominantly have been a place where burials took place outside the medieval town, which would be strange given that there were burial grounds at each of the three churches. Perhaps the stories of soldiers garrisoned in Whiston have some factual basis. It might have been a location where soldiers lived on a temporary basis during times of conflict and where the dead of battle were buried. It certainly seems strange that a burial ground should seemingly contain a large number of burials in an area where there are no records for anyone having lived.

Pottery was produced outside the town defences, in the area of Whiston, as will be outlined in a later chapter. There was also a medieval malt kiln at Huntingdon Street which Alan MacCormick believes to have been associated with Whiston. This would suggest Whiston had more than just a funerary function but with no evidence of habitation it is not currently possible to refer to it as a settlement. It remains an oddity that we can only hope further archaeological work may one day help explain.

Tiggua Cobaucc

(place of the caves)

It has been said that one of Nottingham's hidden secrets is its man-made caves which exist across the city. Whilst this is not quite fair, given that the caves are not actually a secret, they are not known about as well as they might be.

Nottingham was referred to as *Tiggua Cobaucc* in Asser's *Life of King Alfred* written in the late ninth century, which translates as 'place of the caves.'[298] It is possible this was a nickname rather than an official name and there is no evidence to the number or extent of the caves when the reference was made, but clearly Nottingham did have caves during the ninth century.

Nottingham's caves are a major characteristic of the area of the medieval town, and indeed the whole city although the majority of them can be found within the core. Of those outside of the city centre and in the outlying areas such as Radford and Basford, these are generally post-medieval or modern in date. Most are underground but several are visible at ground level, cut into the cliff.

Much has been written about Nottingham's caves, including two recent publications. The first is by Dr Tony Waltham, a leading expert in caves and engineering geology, and is entitled '*The Sandstone Caves of Nottingham*' (originally published in the 1990s but more recently revised) and the second was by Andrew Hamilton, the chair of the Nottingham Civic Society, entitled '*Nottingham's Caves*'. Both should be read but it would be remiss to not include a chapter in this book about these unique and much undervalued features over which thousands of unknowing individuals walk each day. Furthermore, there is much important information which has yet to have been written relating to Nottingham's caves particularly relating to the archaeology of them. It would be quite a simple task to produce an entire book relating to the caves, and for that book to be entirely different to any previously written, but suffice here to produce a relatively small summary of our knowledge of caves as it currently stands. It is my hope that by better understanding the caves we can get a better appreciation of them. It is my further hope that a greater appreciation of them will result in their long term preservation and I am privileged to have worked with the City Archaeologist in helping draft a policy to protect the caves.

There were caves in Nottingham from at least the late Saxon period. However, the locations of these earliest caves (if they survive at all) are unknown, with the earliest dated caves believed to date to c. 1250. Nottingham's caves are difficult to date unless they possess typological features which can be approximately dated, or there is documentation directly relating to cave (which is quite rare and only generally the case for post medieval and modern caves and it is often difficult to distinguish the specific cave referred to in a historic text), or there are artefacts in the deposit used to fill a cave which provide an approximate date as to when it ceased to be used but not when it was first hewn.

By 1609 there must have been hundreds of caves because a document of that year states, 'the whole town is in a manner undermined with caves of an amazing depth and extent, go that it is even questioned whether all the buildings on the surface of the rock would fill up the vacancies underneath.'[299]

Many of the caves have had their appearance, extent and function altered throughout time. Indeed if any of the caves first hewn in Saxon times still survive there is every possibility that they have been enlarged or modified to such an extent that their original outline in plan has been destroyed.

George Campion of the Thoroton Society Excavation Section claimed to have found Saxon caves on the site of the Ice Stadium[300] but his dating appears to be entirely erroneous, and based upon the presence of a Saxon pewter disc or broach in the fill of the cave, which only meant that the cave was backfilled with material which contained one Saxon artefact. This does not necessarily mean the cave had any association to Saxon activity and indeed modern interpretations suggest it was possibly a medieval malt kiln complex.[301] Campion's dating techniques were even more erroneous for the alleged Neolithic cave he thought he had discovered at Low Pavement on the basis of two flints being found in the backfill.[302] It is the same logic as a derelict Victorian house being demolished and its foundations covered in soil which happens to contain a few broken pieces of seventeenth century pottery. The presence of that seventeenth century pottery does not make the house any less nineteenth century in its construction.

Many of the caves were identified and investigated during the Victorian period when development work was being undertaken. We have already seen that Shipman encountered caves during his observations of the railway cutting towards the end of the nineteenth century, and the excavations for a new wing at the General Hospital, and he made notes and some sketch drawings of them. A large number of caves were also found along the full extent of King Street and Queen Street. Thankfully some records were made by Stapleton of many of the caves encountered,[303] but a large number of others across the city centre were destroyed without more than a passing reference and it is to be expected that large numbers of caves were destroyed without any interest being shown in them.

It was not until the twentieth century that the investigation of caves was taken more seriously and had greater popularity. This interest coincided with major redevelopment that allowed the amateur archaeological groups to have the opportunity to explore some of the caves encountered during work associated with, for example, the construction of Maid Marian Way and the Broadmarsh Shopping Centre.

The Thoroton Society Excavation Section, Nottingham Archaeological Society, Peveril Archaeological Group, Nottingham Historical and Archaeological Society and the Hidden History Team are all organisations which have investigated Nottingham's caves on an amateur but enthusiastic and dedicated manner. The Nottingham Historical and Archaeological Society is the only one of these groups

LLTCHER GATE. FROM A SKETCH BY W. STRETTO

A cave drawn in 1819 by William Stretton. It was decorated with crosses, shields and carved heads and is believed, by MacCormick, to have been a medieval maltkiln. Reproduced from the Stretton Manuscript.

A drawing by Clements of part of a medieval cave discovered at 25-31 Warser Gate during the construction of a warehouse in 1890. It was originally believed to be a 'ditch dwelling' but it is now thought to have been a malt kiln complex. (The Author's collection)

still operational and it aims to continue to excavate the caves at the Broadmarsh Shopping Centre, to make more of them accessible to the public.

Professional archaeologists and geologists have, and continue to, excavate and record caves as and when they are encountered on sites and collate information about Nottingham's known caves. The development carried out in the city has led to some caves having to be filled in to enable construction work to commence. This is due to the caves not being known of until groundworks commence. It is not always possible to record caves in such circumstances although developers are duty bound to inform the City Council if a cave is discovered. Usually if a cave is known of some archaeological survey work will be undertaken prior to any development commencing, or at an early stage of development, unless it is too dangerous to do so.

A good example of when construction work encountered caves which had previously been unknown of and which had to be quickly recorded, was on Woolpack Lane when the Habitat building was built. Two caves were encountered, both of which had formed malt kiln complexes (malt kiln complexes will be explained shortly) and dated to the medieval period.[304] Although one had been badly damaged during the construction of a brick building, perhaps in the nineteenth century, they were amongst the best examples of medieval malt kiln complexes in the city and Gordon Young believed them to be the best caves he had ever seen in his more than thirty years of work in Nottingham. It is unfortunate therefore that the caves were filled with concrete and the building work was completed with only a small number of photographs and drawings being produced by John Samuel Archaeological Consultants. The caves could not be preserved because planning permission had already been granted, work had already commenced and unfortunately the best of efforts by Gordon could not stop the work from being carried out, with only a small amount of time being made available to create a record of the caves.

New caves continue to be found and where they are archaeologists should be called to investigate them. The lack of deep stratigraphy for much of the city and the creation of deep cellars and foundations for large buildings has meant that on many sites the only archaeological features that survive are those cut into the rock such as caves.

If a known cave is deemed sufficiently important then any development on the site might only be granted permission if the cave is not affected. Consequently sometimes plans have had to change to ensure a cave is protected, such as at the Broadmarsh Shopping Centre, although some caves were destroyed during the building of it. Some caves will not be deemed sufficiently significant, such as some Victorian cellars, and once they are recorded the development can go ahead and if necessary the cave destroyed, modified or access to it removed.

A number of caves are protected by law either as being part of a Listed Building (such as the extensive cave system at the Guildhall) or as a Scheduled Monument. The caves which are scheduled are those at Lenton Hermitage, all of the caves on the site of Nottingham Castle, part of the Drury Hill caves at the Broadmarsh Shopping Centre, those caves beneath 3–7 Middle Pavement and 8 Castle Gate. These caves will be briefly discussed during the course of this chapter.

In 1979 the archaeologists at the City Council undertook a survey of cellars predominantly around the Lace Market area of Nottingham. This incorporated those caves used as cellars in addition to cellars that are not rock cut. In 1989 the British Geological Survey published its *Register of Nottingham's Caves*, the results of a much more extensive research project of Nottingham's caves which included site visits where possible and archival research. It consisted of an index, a volume consisting of brief descriptions and a volume showing the locations of the caves. In 2004 a volume was published which included additional caves. In 2006 they produced a digitised version of their database with all the caves shown in a map layer for use in a Geographical Information System.

Of the caves recorded by the British Geological Survey it is fair to say that what they have classed as one cave is occasionally in reality several. For example, at King Street and Queen Street they have classed approximately twenty to thirty totally independent caves as being a single cave in their index which they called Ka1. As such the approximately 460 caves in their register are in reality much greater in number.

Between 2008 and 2010 I created the Urban Archaeological Database for Nottingham's historic core which included archival research and inclusion of the results of archaeological fieldwork from reports. During this work, as well as including all caves from the BGS Register, I identified a further approximately sixty caves from work postdating 2004 and some caves the British Geological Survey had missed, bringing the total to approximately 520. Some of these had been destroyed, some survived but were blocked up and others I could not be sure whether they survived or not.

In 2010 Trent & Peak Archaeology began undertaking a survey of Nottingham's caves using 3D laser scanning equipment to produce virtual reality type, detailed images of every cave surveyed. At the time of writing this work is ongoing and it is hoped that a reasonable representative number of various types of cave will be scanned. I worked on the project carrying out archival research to compliment the results of the laser scanning. During this project more caves were identified, particularly along Mansfield Road, and it is anticipated that the list of known caves will grow even further. Indeed during the research of this book I identified more caves, on Mansfield Road, Derby Road and Wheeler Gate, and I have little doubt many more exist.

It is hoped the Nottingham Caves Survey Project, as Trent & Peak Archaeology's project is known, will help raise greater awareness and understanding of the caves, lead the way to bringing large numbers of them into public accessibility and that even some inaccessible caves will be accessible in a virtual reality sense from the comfort of one's home via the Internet. Indeed many caves are already featured on the project's website.

Furthermore Tony Waltham continues to survey caves and use his expertise as an engineering geologist to record caves and where appropriate help minimise the amount of a development's impact upon a cave.

For all the caves which are known there will be many others which exist which people are aware of but do not feature on any records. Furthermore there will be many others which no one knows about, located under buildings but blocked up or located on sites where there is no possibility of knowing they exist. Some of these may one day be revealed when development takes place but then it may be too late to record them or they may be too badly damaged during their discovery.

How many caves once existed but which have been destroyed over the centuries is anyone's guess but I doubt it would be an exaggeration for me to claim that Nottingham has had one thousand caves in as many years. It is likely that the earliest caves were located where the earliest known occupation existed, i.e. in the Lace Market.

Although many caves will have been created by the individuals who used them, with the aid of a pick and other simple tools, it seems likely that there would have been a group of specialist cave diggers. Many caves contain features which are highly decorative, which would have required a great amount of skill. There are also lots of caves which have a resemblance to other caves. Certainly during the nineteenth centuries the decorative caves which will be described later would have been hewn by specialists with skills in stone masonry who were able to craft magnificent looking pillars and other features, some of which bore resemblance to architectural features within Nottingham's churches. Yet surprisingly there is no documentation to show who these individuals were.

The caves in Nottingham were used for vastly varied uses and when functions changed through time the caves would often be enlarged or modified. As such it is not always possible to establish the original function of a cave. It is often the case that we cannot tell what a cave was used for any more than we can establish its age. It is also important to stress here that complexes could have several different functions at the same time or that the functions changed over time.

A myth has emerged that all or most of Nottingham's caves were lived in during early times and indeed there have been tales of druids living in caves such as those at Peel Street and the Broadmarsh Shopping Centre. This is a myth that was popularised by the writings of antiquarians and more recently by George Campion who regularly wrote for the Nottinghamshire Guardian in the 1940s.

However, some caves were indeed lived in, although inhabited caves form only a tiny proportion of cave types.

Sneinton Hermitage, just to the east of the medieval town, consisted of chambers in which people lived. The hermitage was first referred to in 1544 in a rental document which states, 'Item, there is a house under the grounde in a roche of stone that somtyme was called the hermitage.' A later rental document of 1591 refers to 'The Ermytage in Sneynton being a house cutte oute of rock and paieth yearly 2s.'[305]

A drawing by Dr Stukeley of Lenton Hermitage. (Itinerarium Curiosum, 1724)

Several of the caves were destroyed during the nineteenth and early twentieth centuries but some of the chambers still survive and are usually accessible on Heritage Open Days once a year and during an annual festival.

Lenton Hermitage to the west of the medieval town, off Castle Boulevard, was probably the home of two monks from Lenton Priory. From 1244 for a period of twenty years, two monks from the Priory were paid and lived in the chapel of St Mary de la roche, which was the name of the chapel within the Hermitage. It was used in Victorian times as part of a pleasure park and a rock-cut skittle alley can still be seen.[306]

Caves on Hollowstone were cut into the face of the cliff and had been used as dwellings. In 1607 the cave entrances were blocked to prevent them from being lived in.[307]

Yet caves continued to be occupied as pressures on land increased and the cost of living increased coupled with low wages. It is quite likely that some caves were at various points in time used as places for people to live. As family sizes grew it would seem inevitable that any available space would be utilised. An inevitable demand for housing was met by a large supply of caves whose owners could make extra money. A poet by the name of Taylor visited Nottingham in 1639, and wrote, 'A great many of the inhabitants, especially the poorer sort, dwell in vaults, holes, or caves, which are digged out of the rock, so that if a man be destitute of a house, he has only to go to Nottingham, with a mattock, a shovel, a crow of iron, a chisel, a mallet, and with such instruments he may play the mole, the coney, or pioneer, and work himself a hole and a burrow for himself and his family, where over their heads the grass and pasture grows, beasts do feed, and cows are milked.'[308] No doubt there is a degree of poetic license here but it would imply that the poor lived in caves. In the seventeenth century, during a discussion about Sunday recreation in the House of Commons, one of the Members of Parliament for Nottingham told the House that given most of his constituents lived underground recreation time on Sundays should be encouraged. Undoubtedly the Member of Parliament was grossly exaggerating but it would seem clear that there were still a sizeable number of cave dwellers in the seventeenth century. Indeed the problem became a cause for such concern that questions were asked in parliament and in 1845 an Act of Parliament was passed in order to make it illegal to occupy cave cellars.[309]

Perhaps the most obvious function of caves was for storage. The soft sandstone is an ideal material to dig into to produce cellars beneath, or at the rear of (for it should be pointed out that caves were cut both below ground and into the cliff faces) buildings. I will outline some of the most notable examples.

Through documentation we know that on Low Pavement there once stood a building known as Vault Hall, believed to be on the site currently occupied by Gawthorne House (24–26 Low Pavement). First mentioned, as 'Vouthalle', in 1335 the building was named after the extensive caves beneath it which in my opinion were part of the Drury Hill/Broadmarsh caves. The caves were used for the storage of wool.[310]

The adjacent property, known today as Willoughby House and former home of the Willoughby family, has extensive cave cellars beneath the land at the rear of the property and also beneath the building itself. One of the caves is still accessible via a passage which leads to three chambers, each circular in plan, the largest of which has a carved central pillar and table. Deering visited these caves and described this complex as being accessible by 32 steps leading to three

A photograph taken by George Campion of a cave created to be a wine cellar at the rear of Willoughby House on Low Pavement. (Nottingham City Museums and Galleries)

chambers, each with a door. It is known that the caves were originally used for the storage of wine.[311]

In addition to the storage of wine, a more common commodity stored in rock cut cellars was beer. Indeed a large number of public houses that have existed over the centuries have caves beneath them. This is because the sandstone provides a constant cool temperature, ideal for storage of beer. In 1746 a visitor to Nottingham recorded visiting the Flying Horse Hotel where she was taken to the cellars below, which were at 'a surprising depth' with 'several vaults' containing beer. The beer left a great impression on her and she noted how good it tasted!

Most caves used as beer cellars have thralls (benches), either cut out of the rock or constructed of bricks around the sides, to stand barrels on.

Perhaps some of the oldest surviving beer cellars are those beneath the three pubs which compete for the status of Nottingham's oldest; the Trip to Jerusalem, the Salutation Inn and the Bell Inn. Certainly the caves at the Trip to Jerusalem predate the timber building which stands today (which is almost certainly no older than the seventeenth or eighteenth century), though they have probably been extended. It is quite likely the caves do date to the medieval period, when they were associated with the production and storage of beer and water for the castle, although there is no evidence for their existence in 1189; the date given on the side of the building. Those beneath the Salutation

The Trip to Jerusalem, which claims to be England's oldest pub, and which has rock cut chambers which may have been used to provide beer for Nottingham Castle during the medieval period. (The Author)

One of the contenders for Nottingham's oldest pub. Its origins are certainly in the medieval period. (The Author)

are certainly medieval and contain evidence for work having commenced to create further chambers, with the work having been abandoned, probably because they were extending under the street which was an offence punishable by a large fine. These caves are no longer used for the storage of beer. The cellars beneath the Bell Inn (which dendrochronology suggests is probably the oldest of the three pubs) are still used for the storage of beer as they were in medieval times.

Most of the caves outside of the historic core, along Mansfield Road in particular, were originally post-medieval pub cellars and many of them still are today.

Rock cut caves beneath The Salutation, which were used as a beer cellar. (The Author)

Associated with beer is the process of malting. More than thirty cave complexes in Nottingham have been identified as malt kiln systems. The caves, first identified by Alan MacCormick, typically consist of three chambers in trefoil form (i.e. resembling a three leaf clover) consisting of a chamber containing a well to obtain water, a chamber with a central pillar (known as the pillar cave) where malt was spread over the floor and covered in water and left to dry, and the third chamber consisting of a bowl shaped depression which acted as a fire pit over which a wooden platform would be constructed on which malt was heated. A stokehole would lead into the bowl so that the fire could be stoked.[312]

Many of the malt kiln caves had an incised cross, often incised on a pillar, no doubt to request divine protection for those underground whilst the intense fire was burning, to protect the quality of the water in the well and perhaps also to request a good quality malt was produced.

Two of the best surviving examples of malt kiln complexes are those at 8 Castle Gate and 3–7 Middle Pavement, both of which are Scheduled Monuments.

The complex beneath 8 Castle Gate was discovered during groundworks for the Leicestershire Building Society and was excavated by the contractor's labourers but with some archaeological assistance and inspection. The site is now a religious centre. The system, which is almost complete, consists of three chambers in trefoil form, accessed via a central stair down a shaft (the original entrance no longer survives), and is thought to date to c. 1250 which, if correct, makes it one of the oldest known cave systems in Nottingham.[313] Pottery in the backfill dated to the late sixteenth or early seventeenth century suggesting the cave was completely filled in during the early seventeenth century.[314]

According to Deering malting had ceased in Nottingham by the latter part of the reign of Charles I. Charles I's reign was between 1625 and 1649, suggesting that any malt kiln cave must have ceased to be

One of the contenders for Nottingham's oldest pub. Dendrochronology has shown the building is medieval. (The Author)

used for that function by c. 1640.[315] Of course, the caves may still have been used for other purposes after that date. This corresponds nicely with 8 Castle Gate which was perhaps in use until malting ceased.

The cave was dated to c. 1250 by excavating a feature believed to be associated with it. Mid way down the stair into the cave system was another small cave sealed with a stone wall thought, by its style, to date to the fourteenth century. Beyond the wall was a garderobe/latrine pit which contained thirteenth century pottery towards its base.[316] This garderobe would certainly appear to date to the thirteenth century but

A laser scanned image of the Pillar cave part of the 8 Castle Gate malt kiln complex. Image reproduced courtesy of the Nottingham Caves Survey project, Trent & Peak Archaeology.

does not necessarily mean that malting was taking place in the caves system at that time. The malting caves could have been created later. The caves could have existed but were later adapted so they could be used for malting, with the latrine pit then being sealed off from the system. I believe that malting at 8 Castle Gate only began in the fourteenth century.

The malt kiln complex beneath 3–7 Middle Pavement is just part of a large complex of ten chambers. The cave was accessed by steps from the property which led into a square chamber with pillars and thralls. A cave exists either side of these steps. The eastern cave contains a malt kiln. Two wells are present on the site.[317]

Another malt kiln, which is a Scheduled Monument but inaccessible to the public, is beneath the Broadmarsh Shopping Centre and is known as Drury Hill Cave IIIB (on account of it being discovered during the excavations at Drury Hill in trench IIIB). This cave is a small cave complex at approximately 10ft (3m) in diameter with a domed roof and 4ft (1.2m) deep bowl shaped depression surrounded by a rock-cut thrall and is believed to have been in use before the fourteenth century but which possibly fell out of use during the fourteenth century, later becoming a cellar before finally being filled in during the nineteenth century.[318]

One of the caves in the Western Passage at Nottingham Castle was once a malt kiln but was converted to an ice house prior to 1815.[319]

Another industry which some caves were used for was the tanning of hide to produce leather. Some of the caves around the Broad Marsh area of the city were used during late-medieval and early post-medieval period, for tanning. The Pillar Cave complex at Drury Hill and the Black's Head caves both had chambers used as tanneries and will be described here.

Campion excavated part of the Drury Hill cave complex, where he found a large chamber with pits or vats which were used for tanning leather. A further cave had a 10ft (3m) deep well apparently with mud at the bottom containing evidence of tanning. Above this mud were apothecary jars which Campion believed contained ointment used to protect tanners from contracting anthrax.[320]

The caves at Drury Hill were more thoroughly excavated in advance of the construction of the Broadmarsh Shopping Centre. During those excavations evidence was found for tanning during the late-medieval to early post-medieval period. Documentary evidence confirms the caves were used for tanning during the sixteenth and early seventeenth century. The tanning pits comprised of wood with red clay lining and amazingly some scraps of leather were found. A large chamber with a pillar, known as the Pillar Cave, contained four circular clay lined tanning vats with red tile walling, which had been dug into debris from a roof collapse after 1300 and probably before the sixteenth century. It is believed they ceased to be used during the sixteenth century. It was largely due to the surviving evidence of tanning that part of the cave complex was protected by law by being designated a Scheduled Monument.[321]

A complex of six caves was uncovered following subsidence of a yard at the Black's Head on Lister Gate/Low Pavement in 1991. The caves were found to consist of probable seventeenth and eighteenth century cellars, a medieval malt kiln and two caves where tanning had taken place. One of the caves contained parts of fourteen circular and rectangular pits believed to have been tanning vats, approximately 1m deep and some still had evidence of clay lining. The floor was not fully cleared and so further tanning pits may have existed. They had ceased to be used by the late seventeenth or early eighteenth century when the floor of a cellar was constructed which blocked off their access. The caves were filled with concrete for safety reasons.[322]

Some caves have been used as cells to house prisoners. Campion excavated a 'beehive' shaped cave at Cranbrook Street which had a short sloping passageway to a second cave. There was evidence for a heavy door. It was his belief that the cave was a gaol cave with one chamber for the prisoners and a second chamber for the guards.[323] However, this theory can only be found in his private notes and is omitted from the Thoroton Society Excavation Section's Annual Report[324] suggesting that Campion may have changed his opinion or that even he did not think his interpretation was capable of belief. MacCormick believes it was probably a malt kiln complex, although no well was mentioned in Campion's records.[325]

More convincing evidence for gaol cell caves has been found at the Shire Hall (Galleries of Justice) and the old Town Hall where caves were used in medieval and post medieval times to house prisoners, as discussed in a previous chapter.

Much excitement has been aroused at the Galleries of Justice thanks to media reports of a cave said to have been used as 'oubliette' (meaning 'forgotten place') in which Robin Hood may have been kept prisoner before being rescued by Little John, as featured in one of the Ballads of Robin Hood. The chamber exists beneath the extant building and is difficult to gain access to. Consequently it has not yet been excavated and so its function remains uncertain. However, probing of the fill of this cave chamber has shown it does not extend very deep whereas oubliettes have generally been deep pits in which a prisoner could be forced into and forgotten about until they died, with the body remaining in the feature. Nonetheless some of the caves at the Galleries of Justice were used as cells and can be viewed today. What the chamber was used for remains uncertain but hopefully an archaeological excavation may one day help solve this puzzle.

During the excavations for the railway cutting in the late nineteenth century at least five caves used as gaol cells were found on the site of the medieval town hall, which had to be demolished in advance of the railway works. One of these caves had shackles within it. A skeleton of an adult male was also encountered on the site.[326]

A commonly believed myth about Nottingham's caves is that some of them acted as passages leading for miles across the city centre, and often leading to the castle. These stories are largely the result of childhood memories and the passing down of exaggerated stories. The longest cave which could be conceived as a passageway was that on the site of the former General Hospital but even that extended only approximately 100ft (30m) in length, from St James's Street to the hospital site and has never been accessible to the public.[327] Whilst there are extensive caves which have been accessible to the public, such as those at Peel Street, where one could quite easily walk around for several hours and indeed get lost for many an hour (!) even the different access points to the caves are only a matter of metres apart.

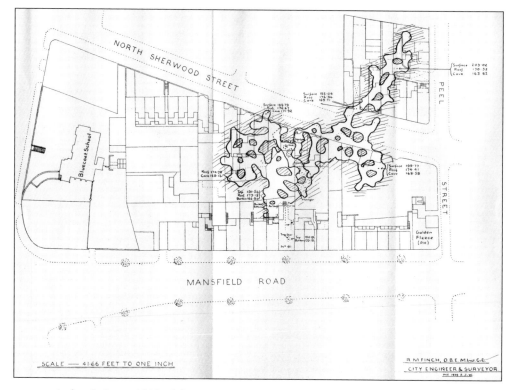

A plan dating to 1939 of the extensive Peel Street caves. (Nottingham City Council)

However, some of the caves were used as passages connecting cave systems or providing an alternative means of entry to a building or garden.

The most notable examples are some of those at the castle which were used in medieval times as a means of transporting people and goods to the castle from the base of the Castle Rock. The caves at the castle are within two separate Scheduled Monuments. The first is that directly beneath the castle grounds as they stand today and the second is those accessed from the base of the Castle Rock, on the south side of the rock.

The most famous is that known as Mortimer's Hole, the 98m long passage popularly believed to have been the means of access to the castle used to capture Roger Mortimer in 1330. Mortimer was the lover of Queen Isabella, wife of King Edward II, and the pair led an invasion against the king which led to Edward being overthrown in 1326. Mortimer was believed to have been responsible for the king's murder.[328]

The story, described by Leland in 1540, claims that one night in October 1330 the 17 year old King Edward III, accompanied by a small group, entered the castle via an underground passageway which was commonly not known about at the time but which a discreet soldier informed the young monarch of. Edward led troops into the castle and found Mortimer with his mother. The couple were seized and Mortimer was taken to the Tower of London and was later executed.

The real Mortimer's Hole probably exists elsewhere on the Castle grounds. The mistake is a result of the Smythson Plan having been

A painting by Thomas Allom, dating to 1836, showing the artist's impression of the young King Edward III leading troops through a tunnel in the Castle Rock to capture Roger Mortimer and Queen Isabella. (Courtesy of the Nottingham City Council and www.picturethepast.co.uk)

annotated at a later time to when it was drawn in 1617. The spiral staircase on the ground, which is still visible today and is used as an access point to the passage, is shown on the plan. Someone has labelled it Mortimer's Hole but this does not mean it is the actual passageway.

The most likely candidate for Mortimer's Hole is that which is known as Davy Scot's Hole (also known as the North-West passage on account of it being located at the north-west of the castle grounds). This is a short passage which runs from the garden of 2 Castle Grove approximately 24m through the Castle Rock to the edge of the Green. The entrance in the Castle Grounds is now covered by shrubs and is sealed. The passage has not been fully investigated but was visited in 1936 when Campion entered part of the tunnel and more recently as part of the Nottingham Caves Survey project. Campion believed it was more extensive than that extent planned by Finch in 1950 but it was partially filled with debris and Campion could not have fully investigated it. The results of geophysics in the 1990s seemed to be in keeping with Finch's plan.

The Western Passage is a 45m long passage accessed from the west of the Castle Rock. In medieval times the passage led into the dry moat at the extreme west and extends to the bottom of the rock. A rock collapse has destroyed the original entrance, which now consists of a concrete frontage. There is an opening to the passage in the cliff face at the rear of a property on Peveril Drive.[329] The passage widens to form a number of chambers, one of which was once a malt kiln but was used as an ice house during the time of Blackner who wrote in 1815.

The passageway has been damaged by wind erosion, with a constant flow of air through the passage which has destroyed many of the tool marks associated with the tunnel's carving. Indeed there is a large amount of sand on the floor throughout the passage where this legally protected monument is being continually damaged. A passage leading from the Western Passage to a cellar associated with the seventeenth century Ducal Palace to store wine was hewn in 1955 to aid cave tours.

Another less common but important post-medieval use for caves was the mining for sand as a building material and for use as part of a floor surface. The cave formed by the process had no function, with the removed material having importance but the voids could later be used for storage.[330]

The most notable of these sand mines is beneath land off Peel Street, covering approximately 120m in length by 80m in width. The caves were created by James Rouse who mined them for sand in the late eighteenth century for approximately thirty years. The caves consist of many winding passages with rock-cut and brick pillars (the latter installed during the system's later use as an air raid shelter) and a manger near one of the entrances for a horse. It is such an extensive system that it is unsurprising many a person has got lost in the caves.[331]

Another sand mine system exists on the opposite side of Mansfield Road, running beneath land belonging to numbers 208 and 216.[332]

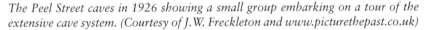

The Peel Street caves in 1926 showing a small group embarking on a tour of the extensive cave system. (Courtesy of J.W. Freckleton and www.picturethepast.co.uk)

Slightly further south, but still off Mansfield Road, could once be found what Waltham calls the Whiston Mines. This was a small complex of caves on the east side of Mansfield Road, close to the Peel Street sand mine caves. They are believed by Waltham to have been sand mines on the basis of their appearance and close proximity to the other sand mines. They were filled with concrete in the 1980s.[333]

There has always been a desire amongst society's wealthiest to use elaborate architecture to display their wealth and status. This is especially apparent in Nottingham's caves during the Victorian period.

One of the best examples of the use of caves to display wealth and status are those found on the Ropewalk. In 1872 Alderman Thomas

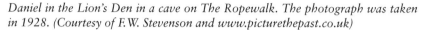

Daniel in the Lion's Den in a cave on The Ropewalk. The photograph was taken in 1928. (Courtesy of F. W. Stevenson and www.picturethepast.co.uk)

Herbert had caves, known as the grottos, carved. The caves survive today and are an impressive sight, though unfortunately not open to the public. They consist of two adjacent caves, one of which had a tunnel running from the Alderman's garden, to a garden now belonging to a property on Park Terrace but which also belonged to Herbert. The passage has a number of pillars and leads to a cave chamber with other carved features including a sphinx, druids and what is known as Daniel and the Lion's Den; a carved figure of Daniel playing a harp with two lions beside him. Unfortunately vandals removed one of the lion's heads and part of the carving of Daniel in recent decades.[334]

The second cave was originally carved as a summer house, but later turned into a grotto. Various animals are represented amongst the carvings in this chamber, including snakes, birds and crocodiles. A further elaborate feature is a rock cut staircase replicating that at Haddon Hall in Derbyshire.[335]

A large rectangular cave at Maria Court, off Fishpond Drive, is another example of the use of Victorian elaborate sculpture within a cave. Two life size human figures, believed by Waltham to possibly represent Samson and Moses, a large sofa and a lion were carved. The cave also had windows cut into the front of the cliff face.[336]

Another example of Victorian extravagance, which ultimately proved to be a waste of money in that it failed to achieve its original purpose, is that known as the Park Tunnel.

The Duke of Newcastle desired that he should have a tunnel used for his horse and carriage linking The Park to Derby Road, so that he could avoid the steep hill. Work on the tunnel commenced in 1840 but probably due to the high costs and labour involved it was abandoned, only being completed fifteen years later. However, when finished the gradient of the passage was found to be too steep for the horses and so it was not used.[337]

A cave system beneath the castle (and part of the Scheduled Monument) has been used as a rifle range in recent decades. It can be entered from Castle Road and extends to underneath the castle's bandstand. It consists of a number of probable post medieval chambers with seventeenth or eighteenth century brick partitions, with twentieth century passages leading off them. The passages are of varying lengths, probably for the use of different types of rifle, and were created by heavy duty mining equipment. When a building on Castle Road, known as Rock House, was demolished in January 1928 the caves behind it were investigated. Only the probable post-medieval chambers were noted.[338] The passages were also not on a plan drawn in 1904 of the castle and its caves although the chambers fronting Castle Road were drawn. So clearly the passages are more recent than 1928 but were in existence by 1941 when they were used as air raid shelters during the war and were drawn on air raid shelter survey cards. It is unclear exactly when they were created but I suspect they were hewn in anticipation of, or in the early stages of, the Second World War.

It is amazing that there is no known record relating to the creation of something made within living memory, at such a prominent location where the drilling equipment would have been seen, but this is a theme found elsewhere in Nottingham. In fact there was a cave used as a studio by the well known Nottingham artist Laura Knight during the early twentieth century. The cave was known as the Castle Studios, if only by the artist herself, but its location is unknown. There is no cave known to have existed anywhere near the castle which matches the quite detailed description given in Knight's autobiography.

One of the most common uses of the caves, although by and large not the original use for them, was during the Second World War when large numbers of the caves were adapted and used as air raid shelters although some new caves were created for this purpose. Official records state that by February 1941, eighty-six caves were used as public shelters but I dare say that others were used too, especially any beneath private residences. The cave shelter at the Player's Factory in Radford was undoubtedly the largest purpose built shelter, and could accommodate 8896 people.

Campion wanted the Corporation to create an entire city underground by extending pre-existing caves and carving new ones to ensure safety during heavy bombing raids.

Although caves were used as air raid shelters during the Second

World War there is evidence that at least one was used during the First World War. A cave on the site of the Ice Stadium car park is claimed to have been used as Nottingham's first air raid shelter during a Zeppelin raid in 1916. Inscriptions on one of the walls of the cave are to the effect.[339]

During the height of the Second World War, and the beginning of the Cold War, with concerns of nuclear attack, the caves beneath the Guildhall were modified to act as a civil defence headquarters for Nottingham's official and key emergency personnel.[340]

There were hopes in the 1970s of creating an underground 'road of the future' to rectify the damage caused by the creation of Maid Marian Way which divided the city centre. It was hoped with traffic travelling underground, the original roads could be reinstated and the city would become more attractive. The project was deemed too costly and got little further than the concept stage.[341]

Today in addition to their use as cellars, some caves are used as tourist attractions and there are hopes to increase the number of caves accessible to the public. One property developer hopes to connect many of the caves together to produce a unique tourist attraction, though even if permission was granted for such a scheme it would prove extremely expensive and labour intensive.

Caves are currently open to the public at the castle, the Museum of Nottingham Life at Brewhouse Yard, the Broadmarsh Shopping Centre, the Galleries of Justice, occasionally Lenton Hermitage and Sneinton Hermitage and under a number of pubs by arrangement with their management. There are hopes of opening up more caves to the public but in the meantime many can be viewed from the comfort of your own home via the Nottingham Caves Survey Project website.

Industry

Nottingham is best known, in terms of industry, for its lace manufacturing which began in the late eighteenth century. However, it has a long tradition of a wide range of industries stemming back at least a thousand years, and those which took place in Saxon and medieval times will be outlined here.

There was a significant increase in the wealth of the town following the Norman Conquest. By 1086, according to Domesday, the town's contribution in tax had risen from £18 to £30 and the mint had increased from £2 to £10 in value, suggesting a significant increase in the economic wellbeing following the conquest, although some of this increase must be attributed to William the Conqueror's harsh fiscal policies. By the end of the eleventh century the Great North Road, referred to in Domesday, passed through Nottingham and through Sherwood Forest. Its origins may have been in the ninth century, when Nottingham and York were important Danish settlements, with the need for communication and trade links between the two. Along with the Trent, this road ensured Nottingham's trading importance during the late Saxon and post-Conquest periods, with trade being one of the greatest contributors to the economy. Forty-eight merchant houses are referred to in Domesday but trade would have been taking place during the Saxon period.[342] This ability to trade encouraged the growth of industry within Nottingham.

One of the key industries from Saxon times through to the eighteenth century was pottery production and the production of ceramic floor and roof tiles. Within the area bounded by the medieval defences were a number of pottery and tile kilns during the late Saxon and medieval periods. Contrary to what some have believed, few kilns have actually been found but their presence in history can be inferred by the discovery of large amounts of pottery wasters – fragments of rejected pottery if you will that were damaged during the firing process in the kiln – showing that one or more kilns had existed nearby and the vessels which failed or were not up to standard were simply thrown away. Whilst the presence of a few pottery wasters would not necessarily mean a kiln was nearby, because sherds of pottery can be transported as soil is moved, a large amount of pottery wasters in a small area does indicate a kiln in the immediate vicinity because pottery waste would have been disposed of very close to the kiln (there would be little benefit in moving it very far).

Part of a tenth century pottery kiln was found during the excavations at Halifax Place. Unfortunately the kiln was on the edge of the excavated area and so only part of it could be exposed and investigated. It was believed to have produced cooking pots, bowls and storage vessels.[343]

Splashed Ware pottery made in Nottingham, on display at Nottingham Castle (The Author)

A pottery kiln which produced splashed ware pottery between c. 1225-1250, truncated by a nineteenth century cellar wall, as excavated by Charles Young, at Goose Gate. (Nottingham City Museums and Galleries, NCMG 2013–7)

The pottery types produced by the Halifax Place kiln are not known to have been encountered elsewhere in Nottingham or further afield, according to pottery expert Vicky Nailor who worked as the pottery specialist on the Big Six excavations.[344] The kiln's association with large, presumably high status buildings discussed in an earlier chapter has led to the suggestion that on site manufacture for a single household or small number of households of tremendous importance took place.

Two medieval pottery kilns were found at Goose Gate during excavations in 1976. One of the kilns had been rebuilt, repaired and relined several times. The kilns produced pitchers, jugs, cooking pots, bowls and pipkins between c. 1225 and 1250.[345]

A large dump of pottery, including wasters of green glazed pottery, was found on the west side of Western Street in 1936 whilst extending a shop. Campion believed this was evidence of pottery manufacture nearby during the fifteenth century.[346]

Seventy years later further work at Western Street was undertaken by Trent & Peak Archaeology. Fragments of a kiln, possibly tile-lined, and a large number of pottery wasters were found during an excavation and watching brief at the northern end of the street. A number of pits contained wasters of high quality vessels including glazed jugs (which formed the main item of production), unglazed jars and cooking pots that had been produced by the kiln which is believed to have been operational between c. 1250 and 1325. There was evidence that splashed ware pottery had been produced on the site at an earlier time, but this was uncertain.[347] Campion's dating was wrong or there may have been a longer period of pottery production in the area.

Two kilns which appeared to have been used to make pottery and tiles during the medieval period were found by George Campion on land just east of the Parliament Street and Broad Street junction, adjoining the New Market Hotel in 1932. There was also evidence in the form of glass waste, cinder and part of a glass crucible, to show that glass production has taken place in the area in post medieval times, after the pottery and tile kilns had ceased to be used. Indeed a glasshouse had been in operation nearby, on the site of where the

Victoria Shopping Centre now stands and which gave its name to Glasshouse Street. Soil from the glasshouse area had clearly been used to bury the kilns.[348]

Evidence for a pottery kiln was found during an evaluation excavation at 5 George Street undertaken by Wessex Archaeology. A brick and tile built flue was recorded and a large number of pottery wasters were recovered. The kiln was thought to date to the fourteenth or fifteenth century. A watching brief undertaken by John Samuels Archaeological Consultants on the junction of George Street and Old Lenton Street found a cave containing late thirteenth to early fourteenth century pottery kiln waste and tile fragments.[349]

In 1816 during the digging of foundations for a Methodist Chapel on Lower Parliament Street an 'immense' quantity of broken 'monastic paving tiles' and a large amount of mainly unglazed 'ancient' pottery wasters was discovered, according to Stretton, suggesting pottery and tile kilns had been operating in the area during medieval times.[350]

In 1874 further work was undertaken on the site, with more discoveries relating to the kiln. More sherds of pottery and broken floor and roof tiles were encountered, which were believed to date to the fourteenth century. The pottery wasters represented fragments of cooking pots and bowl. Green glazed pots and jugs were also found along with thirteenth and fourteenth century coins.[351] There was no actual kiln encountered although it was described as a kiln site. Unfortunately many who have found pottery dumps have described finding a kiln when this is simply not true.

During the excavation of the Great Central Railway, at Clinton Street in 1897, a kiln was recorded as having been found at a depth of between 10 and 12ft (3–3.7m). A number of squat pitchers and wasters were found and fragments of jug, 'stew jars', butter pots and drinking vessels. Several complete or almost complete pots were stacked on top of one another. The pottery was believed to date to the fourteenth or fifteenth century.[352] However, this was not a kiln. There was no evidence of a kiln structure and it was instead simply a pottery dump in a pit or well. Nonetheless, it suggested a kiln existed nearby.

Interestingly there has been a large amount of evidence for

medieval pottery manufacture outside the medieval town, north of the defences on land bounded by Parliament Street, Mansfield Road and Huntingdon Street, extending as far north as St Ann's Street in the area where Whiston existed in the fourteenth and possibly thirteenth centuries.

A medieval pottery kiln was found in 1939 on Union Road and Glasshouse Street with a large dump of green glazed pottery sherds associated with it.[353]

In 1970 Bob Alvey found three pits containing a very large amount of pottery wasters at St Ann's Street, though there was certainly no evidence of the kilns which produced the material, contrary to what has been written in the past. Certainly at least one pottery kiln must have existed nearby, with the pits being created to dispose of the waste.[354]

The locations of the pottery kilns and other evidence of pottery manufacture are interesting because much of the medieval pottery making took place outside of the medieval town defences. Why was this? Was it due to the prevailing wind? If so why was other industry carried out within the town defences? Given that the Beck ran through the area of the pottery production, it might be that the potters located themselves there for a supply of water and clay which was unavailable in the town. It is worth considering. Another point worth considering is the relationship between the pottery production and Whiston. Perhaps they were connected.

Unfortunately the dating of the pottery and the kilns is not usually good enough to accurately show when the kilns were in use. This is often because the pottery was dated by amateur archaeologists, antiquarians or even professional archaeologists whose knowledge and resources may have been inadequate to establish close dating and the artefacts no longer survive. Usually the antiquarian records only described pottery as medieval, a period which covers almost 500 years and even with such vagueness they may not have always been correct. It should therefore be emphasised that some of the dates given above, particularly those relating to the earliest discoveries, might be wrong. As such we cannot establish which areas had pottery production at any one time, and how the distribution of pottery kilns changed over time, which is unfortunate. It would have been especially useful to know when pottery production commenced outside the confines of the medieval town.

If the pottery outside the town was associated with Whiston then perhaps the pottery production outside the medieval town began and ended at the same time as Whiston is believed to have existed (during the late thirteenth and early fourteenth centuries), but this is merely supposition.

The tanning of leather was another important industry during the late-medieval and early post medieval period. The use of caves for tanning at Drury Hill and Lister Gate/Low Pavement has already been mentioned but there was other tanning activity which took place above ground close to the River Leen. Tanning is a process which required access to water, hence why it was concentrated around the Narrow Marsh part of Nottingham, close to the Leen. It is a foul smelling activity, involving putrefaction of cattle hides and the use of urine to soak the hides in, which is probably why it was carried out in caves where ever possible and around Narrow Marsh which was a poor, overcrowded slum area in medieval times up until as recent as the early twentieth century.

During the construction of the Great Central Railway towards the end of the nineteenth century, and on other occasions, a writer named Granger visited excavations at Cliff Road (known then as Narrow Marsh). A large number of horns and other animal parts were found at depths of at least 10ft (3m). Excavations on the north side of the canal revealed 'black' soil containing horns and other cattle remains. The animal remains were believed to be associated with the tanning process in that they represented the animals whose hides were tanned to form the leather.[355]

During an archaeological evaluation by Northamptonshire Archaeology in 2006 as part of the plans to redevelop the Broadmarsh Shopping Centre, a large quantity of tarsal and metatarsal from cattle were found in thirteenth to fifteenth century deposits near Canal Street and in the southern limit of where the Grey Friar's friary had existed, close to the Leen. It was believed this represented further evidence of the tanning industry.[356]

It has been said that Nottingham had a mint from the tenth century until the thirteenth century but unfortunately no trace has been found of where the mint was located. However, there is evidence of other metal production sites in the historic core.

During excavations at Boots Garage, on Woolpack Lane a late-Saxon smelting hearth was uncovered.[357] There is a lack of other evidence for metalworking during the Saxon period, however.

The evidence for medieval metal working is centred around the High Pavement area, close to St Mary's Church. During excavations on the site of Halifax Place residual tap slag and smelting slag were recovered from some of the excavated features suggesting iron smelting may have occurred in the vicinity of the site.[358] Excavations on the site of the Old High Pavement School revealed industrial debris possibly dating to the mid to late fifteenth century. This consisted of coal ash, coarse clay moulds and bronze slag with lead content. The moulds in particular suggested mortars or cauldrons had been manufactured nearby during this period.[359]

Also on High Pavement, at the Galleries of Justice, smithing slag and hammerscale were found in a charcoal rich layer during archaeological work by Trent & Peak Archaeology in advance of, and during, renovations. All phases of occupation seemed to contain slag and hammer scale suggesting that smithing had taken place nearby throughout much of the medieval and post-medieval period.[360]

At Garner's Hill, at the junction of High Pavement and Middle Hill, eight pieces of slag, twenty-three or twenty-four pieces of slag/debris and one piece of slag/pot were found suggesting metalworking had taken place on or very near the site during the medieval period.[361]

It appears then that all medieval metal production currently known about, took place in the south of the medieval town in the English borough. This may be because metal smelting requires a good supply of air to fuel the furnace and produces much smoke and so the higher land around St Mary's Church would be an appropriate site. The area was also close to the River Leen which would have been an essential means of transporting raw materials to the smelters. Of course it could also have occurred elsewhere and the evidence has been destroyed but it is my personal belief that the High Pavement area was the metalworking centre of medieval Nottingham.

Malting has already been mentioned in an earlier chapter in relation to the use of some caves as malt kiln complexes. All known maltings were below ground and more than thirty caves have been identified so far as having been used for this process, supposedly dating as far back as c. 1250 but quite possibly being created later in the medieval period.[362] However, this is not to say there were no malt kilns above ground. Certainly I have excavated malt kilns in Leicester which were above ground. Nottingham is known to have had kilns to dry corn (corn-dryers) above ground and so there is no reason why they could not have created a kiln for malt above ground too.

Nonetheless only malt kiln caves are known of and all but one of these are located in the medieval town; the exception being that beneath 240 Huntingdon Street which MacCormick believes may have been associated with Whiston.[363] As stated in an earlier chapter, malting ended during the latter part of the reign of Charles I (who reigned between 1625 and 1649), according to Deering. Contrary to what has been written by some in the past, malting was not exclusively a medieval function of the caves.

Holes in the ground which vaguely resemble keyholes or a figure of 8 in plan are encountered on many archaeological sites. These are often ovens created for drying corn. These corn dryers in Nottingham were usually above the ground, cut into the bedrock, and have a wicker superstructure, although some possible corn dryers have been found in caves.

Corn dryers have been found at several sites in Nottingham. An excavation at St Mary's Gate by Birmingham Archaeology revealed several large ovens. A corn drying kiln predating c. 1225–50 was found at Goose Gate, and eight corn dryers were found at Halifax Place dating to before 1250.[364]

Earlier such ovens have also been found. At Fisher Gate two tenth or eleventh century corn drying ovens were found. The ovens had timber flues and domed wicker structures daubed with clay, over the rock cut depression. A large amount of charred corn husks were found in one of the ovens, which had burnt down whilst being used. Attempts were made to put the fire out but by the time the flames were extinguished the oven and its contents were destroyed. At Boots Garage a small late-Saxon or Saxo-Norman corn drying oven was found. Evidence of its timber and wicker structure was also found.[365]

Clearly then, archaeology has provided a reasonable amount of detail about the industries of Nottingham's Saxon and medieval past.

The Civil War

The Civil War is a period which is often forgotten in terms of Nottingham's past, yet its importance was great during the period of conflict and archaeology has provided some relevant information.

Historic sources show that Nottingham's involvement in the Civil War was significant. It was near the castle, on Standard Hill, that Charles I raised the Royal Standard giving the call to arms which commenced the conflict. The castle and the town were captured by the Parliamentarians and the castle was slighted during the conflict, being demolished soon after the hostilities ceased. Lucy Hutchinson wrote the memoirs of her husband who was governor of the town, providing great detail of Nottingham, the castle and the activities of the Civil War albeit from a biased point of view, and based upon her recollections.

The reader will no doubt by now realise that it is almost always impossible to accurately date (to within a period of a year or even a few years) anything encountered on an archaeological excavation and so approximate dates have to be given unless documentary sources provide a date. However, given that we know the castle was unoccupied for much of the seventeenth century until the outbreak of the Civil War, and it was destroyed soon afterwards, anything encountered relating to occupation and activity around the mid seventeenth century is likely to be associated with the hostilities.

Excavations at the castle have revealed some changes to the structure, which were associated with the castle's use during the war. There were signs of repair to make the derelict structure more fit for purpose as a defensive against attack. It has been said in a previous chapter that the castle was ruinous and indeed Lucy Hutchinson described it as such when she wrote, 'the buildings were very ruinous and unhabitable, neither affording roome to lodge souldiers nor provisions.' She described that several towers had existed, 'but the

An artist's impression of the raising of the Royal Standard, under the supervision of King Charles I, close to Nottingham castle, signifying the start of the English Civil War. Reproduced from Deering, 1740.

most of them were downe ... the walls were all downe. ... There were the ruins of in old paire of gates, with turrets on each side.' The castle had few defensive features, with only 'a little brestworke, before the outmost gate', when Hutchinson assumed control of it. [366]

The repairs were undertaken quickly upon Hutchinson's arrival at the castle. Hutchinson made a proclamation to the townspeople calling for them to lodge at the castle so that they be protected, on condition that they assist with reparations. Around 400 took up the offer but many refused to give up their homes.[367]

In Richard's Tower graffiti was found which was believed to have been created by soldiers garrisoned in the castle who wished to leave their mark and the skeleton of a male was found in the Castle Green, who may have been a casualty of the conflict or who at least probably died during the war.[368]

A 'lion's den' dungeon was used, according to Lucy Hutchinson, to house Royalist prisoners,[369] though it is uncertain which cave was used.

St Nicholas' Church was destroyed during the Civil War in 1643 to prevent further bombardment of the castle. The remains were pulled down in 1647. Archaeology has shown evidence for the destruction although it cannot be closely dated so thankfully we have documentary evidence for this. St Peter's Church was also damaged but again we only have documentary evidence for this.[370]

In addition to the castle, defences were created around the town and these have been the subject of antiquarian and archaeological research and investigation. During the Civil War, new gates or doors were fitted at Chapel Bar, some streets were blocked off seemingly with large stones to prevent access, the Leen Bridge was demolished and a drawbridge was constructed over the Leen close to the castle.[371]

In March 1644 a small fort was built by the Parliamentarians to protect the dams in the Meadows area from Royalist attack. It is known as Hooper's Sconce, after its designer. It was described as being in 'the midst of the meadows' by Lucy Hutchinson.[372]

Although archaeological work has failed to locate the sconce, Deering noted seeing an area of raised land between the Trent Bridge and the Castle, in the Meadows, which did not flood. He believed this was the site of the sconce and that it was therefore located south of a bridge which stood over the Tinker's Leen near to where the west end of Traffic Street is today.[373]

Two further forts were created, one being a small fort at the Trent Bridge built by the Royalists which was held by the Royalists for three weeks before being captured and used by the Parliamentarians before being recaptured in April 1645. A second fort was built by the Parliamentarians, possibly in April 1645 during the siege by the Royalists, and was probably located immediately north of the Trent Bridge.[374] Archaeology has failed to locate these forts so their locations can only be guessed.

Defensive ditches and bulwarks were constructed leading from the castle to the north of the post-medieval town, according to Lucy Hutchinson, towards the end of 1642 and were demolished in October

1647. By the beginning of July 1643 Nottingham had 'large workes made about it which would have requir'd at least three thousand men to man and defend them well.'[375] There were approximately fourteen guns situated on these works. The works were described as being 'half moones and bulwarkes.'[376] Their precise locations are unknown although Shipman claimed he and his brother had seen stretches of an 'ancient ditch' which Butler, writing for the Thoroton Society in 1949, interpreted as being the Civil War defences.[377] It has also been suggested any ditch might have been used to defend the town during the later Jacobite Rebellion of 1745–46. Shipman recorded various sections of what he believed were ditches and joined them together to form a projection of an 'ancient ditch.' On numerous occasions Shipman actually identified two ditches close to one another suggesting that the defences may have consisted of at least two ditches running parallel to one another. The inner ditch was 16ft (4.9m) wide and 7ft (2.1m) deep, the outer ditch, 20ft (6.1m) beyond, was 8ft wide (2.4m) and 5ft (1.5m) deep.[378]

However, archaeological work suggests that Shipman's projection is completely wrong. Watching briefs at Goldsmith Street and during work at the Newton Building of Trent University, failed to locate any ditches yet they should have passed through both sites if Shipman was correct and would have been visible due to their size if they were present. Only a small dyke on the line of a mapped nineteenth century field boundary was seen at the Newton building.[379] So, where were the ditches seen by Shipman? Did he instead note several field boundary ditches and believe they were part of a large 'ancient' ditch? Or did he see only minor short features in the small holes he looked in? If Shipman and Butler were wrong, where is the Civil War ditch referred to by Lucy Hutchinson?

In my opinion the post-Conquest ditch would have been dug out once again to create the defences, with a bank also produced. It would be much easer to dig soil out of a ditch that had been filled in, rather than carve out a new defensive ditch out of rock. Of course, during the seventeenth century the town did expand beyond the medieval defences but Lucy Hutchinson's book does state that the people of Nottingham were encouraged to move inside the town and in particular to the castle.

There is evidence of the medieval ditch being used in the Civil War.

An excavation of the post-Conquest ditch at Park Row showed it had been re-cut during the seventeenth century.[380] At Fisher Gate the excavation by Charles Young revealed a major ditch dating to the seventeenth century, which is thought to have possibly been part of a Civil War defence.[381] Elsewhere the post-Conquest ditch has not been fully investigated by archaeologists. It was mainly encountered during the Victorian period by antiquarians such as Shipman who were more interested in the town wall. At Theatre Square the edge of the ditch was encountered but it could not be investigated due to health and safety concerns.

In addition to the defences it has been said that a number of burials found near the castle were associated with the Civil War. A hill on the site later occupied by the General Hospital was levelled in the eighteenth century and during this work 'several' human skeletons were found. The bodies were buried 'promiscuously' together and appeared as if they had been slain in battle and hurriedly disposed of. One skull bore what appeared to be a bullet hole. A dagger, coin and token (dated 1669) were found associated with the burials.[382] It has often been claimed the skeletons were the battle dead of the Civil War but the 1669 half penny token must surely cast doubt on such a belief, given that the war had ended more than twenty years earlier.

Interestingly Thoroton, whose work was published in 1677 and who was writing his manuscript in the years before, did not mention any burials, yet he referred to the area. Thoroton described how a windmill had stood on Derry Mount at the time,[383] although he was probably mistaken with another hill in close proximity to Derry Mount having been known as Windmill Hill. Deering also believed Derry Mount was used for a windmill but his source of information was probably Thoroton's book. It has also been suggested that Derry Mount was created during the Civil War but was only as a platform for ordinance. Lucy Hutchinson described such a hill being created, 'The governor also caus'd a mount neere the castle to be bulwark'd.'[384]

Under what circumstances the skeletons came to be interred in Derry Mount is yet another mystery in need of resolution, as is the mystery of a number of burials discovered two centuries later at Cranbrook Street.

The Cranbrook Conundrum

In 2008 I was made aware of a number of human skeletons found just outside the Lace Market almost half a century previously. I undertook a large amount of research of the discoveries, which had never before been written up, and produced a paper which was published in 2011 in The Transactions of the Thoroton Society of Nottinghamshire.[385] However, I believe it is important to produce here a summary of the site and any conclusions, because I believe it is a highly important site which is still very much a mystery and would interest a wider readership.

In July 1962 James Leonard Beeson, a labourer, discovered human skeletal remains on a development site of office blocks on Lower Parliament Street whilst looking "for anything interesting". He found a human vertebra, nine fragments of skull, two pelvic bones and a jawbone complete with teeth. It was widely speculated that they were the remains of a victim of the Cholera outbreak of 1832 who had been buried in a plague pit.[386]

The following year Tony Wass directed fieldwork, with the assistance of members of the Thoroton Society, between 3 and 17 March 1963 prior to the construction of Cranbrook House on land fronting Lower Parliament Street and Cranbrook Street.

Wass extended Beeson's test pit to a maximum extent of 13ft 6 inches (4.1m) by 5ft (1.5m) with a depth of at least 3ft (0.9m) and revealed parts of twelve human skeletons, with a stray skull possibly having belonged to a skeleton close by which was minus a skull. Only one skeleton (the one minus a skull) was fully excavated. None of the skeletons and partial skeletons was orientated. Some were lying on top of one another at different angles as if they had been hurriedly buried.

When the site was fully stripped by the contractors further skeletal remains, allegedly representing approximately sixty individuals, were

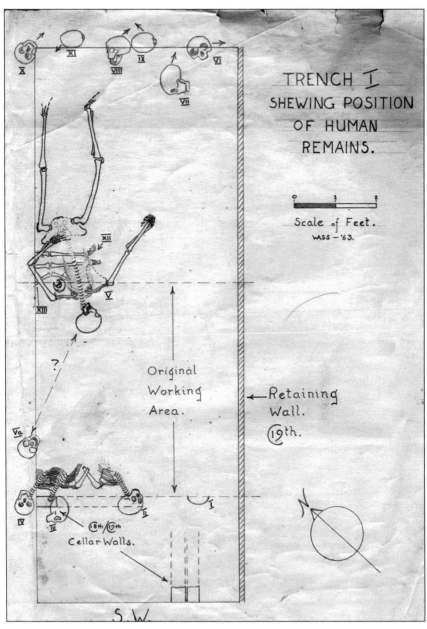

A plan drawn by Tony Wass of the trench he excavated at Cranbrook House in which human remains were discovered. (Nottingham City Museums and Galleries)

A photograph of one of the skeletons found at Cranbrook House. (Nottingham City Museums and Galleries)

uncovered, with a higher concentration towards the south of the site (Cranbrook Street frontage), but with a higher concentration of 'disarticulated skulls' towards the north (Parliament Street).

Another clue to the puzzle could be found three decades further into history than Wass' discovery. In 1935 an exhibition was held showing photographs of 'early burials' found at Lennox Street, thought to be possibly associated with the burial ground of St John's Hospital.[387] It will soon be shown they were not associated with St John's hospital burial ground but their close proximity to Cranbrook House site means they were probably associated with those burials. Unfortunately no further details of the Lennox Street finds, or the photographs, could be located during my research despite a search through the County Archives.

So clearly there was a site was a large number of burials that had never featured in any of Nottingham's history books and was little known about before my research.

Unfortunately Wass' records are so piecemeal, with vague details, few photographs (which were only developed in 2010 and are poor quality) of only part of the site. This has made it difficult to assess how accurate many of Wass' records and interpretations are.

So, how old are the skeletons and why were they buried in that hurried way?

The site was just outside the pre-Conquest borough but within the medieval town. During his excavation Wass identified what he believed were 'clearly defined seventeenth, eighteenth and nineteenth ground levels.' He did not cite any evidence for how he could 'clearly' define this stratigraphy, however. Wass believed they predated an eleventh or twelfth century accumulation, and could have been as early as the ninth century, and were the victims of epidemic or conflict hurriedly thrown into a pond or marshland which he believed existed on the site. He dated the eleventh or twelfth century accumulation on the basis of pottery he thought to be of that period within the layer.

The only artefact recovered, during Wass' excavation, which was directly associated with the skeletons, was an iron irregular crescent shaped object which Gordon Young believes may have been a small horse shoe. When I viewed it, it was fragmented and badly corroded and so I could not establish what its function was. It is of unknown date.

Wass' reference to a pond or marshland was based on the antiquarian belief that there was flooding in the area of Cranbrook Street but also because he found a band of 'dirty sand and silt' immediately below the skeletons containing twigs, leaf mould, grass and 'the like.' Beneath this were layers of graded pebbles and gravels.

Unfortunately Wass did not record the extent of this organic material although he did note that the stratigraphy of approximately half of the development site was similar to that he had excavated within his trench, though there is no further reference to organic material.

An earlier chapter states the potential evidence for waterlogged deposits in this area. However, there is the possibility that the organic material cited by Wass, which is not visible in the photographs albeit that they are poor quality, was the consequence of contamination. Given that Beeson dug a hole in the site in 1962 and removed some human remains, a hole which Wass then extended, it is possible that some organic material got into the hole during this time. It is a common feature of every excavation site which is left open for more than a short time. Wass' plan, if it can be believed, shows that the labourer's test pit had caused some disturbance to the human remains he encountered. Indeed two skulls are lying on top of eighteenth and nineteenth century foundations of buildings which were only demolished in the twentieth century. So clearly if the human remains could be disturbed slightly then it is possible contamination could have taken place. However, that does not explain the widespread disorientated remains elsewhere on the site. It just explains that Wass' belief in a waterlogged site may not have been based on accurate information.

A modern date for the organic material seems likely but this does not necessarily mean there was no tract of marshland or pond, and does not mean that the skeletons are of no great age.

They could not have been associated with St John's burial ground because that was on the grounds of St John's Hospital which was outside the town wall, so it would seem unlikely that the Cranbrook House discoveries were on the site of the land used for the medieval burials of the hospital, or that there was any direct association with the hospital.

Given that only one burial was found on the site of St John's Hospital when the prison was constructed, could the burials have been moved to Cranbrook House? It is theoretically possible but the articulation of some of the skeletons seems to rule this out. Also it would be unusual for the burials to be relocated inside the town when there was so much empty space outside the town. Furthermore, there had been so little development on the site of the St John's Hospital from the time it ceased to have burials until the time the prison was constructed and so there would have been no need to have moved any burials.

Could the burials have been the result of an epidemic? Historic maps show there were houses and courts occupying the site by 1820 and therefore the site could not have had burials twelve years later. They were therefore not associated with the first Cholera outbreak of 1832 or indeed any subsequent visitation of the disease. There was an outbreak of smallpox in 1736 but historic texts and maps show a cherry orchard on the site in c. 1740 and it is highly unlikely that its owner, John Sherwin, would have wanted to grow cherry trees on the site of a large number of infected bodies which had only recently been interred.

Interestingly Deering did not record any known burials when writing his history in c. 1740, despite describing his knowledge of the Cranbrook Street area, and neither did Thoroton (whose work was published in 1677), suggesting that the skeletons were not of a time within the living memories of these two antiquarians and their contemporaries.

No epidemic is known to have taken place during the medieval period that would have required so many burials. That is not to say they were not the victims of an epidemic, however.

If they were victims of an epidemic it still does not explain how a higher concentration of skulls was present at one end of the site compared to the other, if Wass' records were correct, because burials would have taken place whilst the bodies were fully articulated and so skulls should not have been displaced.

Could the burials have been a remnant of Civil War conflict? Nottingham's role during the Civil War, and the activities within the town during the hostilities, has been well documented, most notably by Lucy Hutchinson in her biography of her husband, Colonel Hutchinson who was Governor of Nottingham.

The sources show there was comparatively little fighting and few deaths in Nottingham, with certainly no record of such a large number of deaths as seventy. Lucy Hutchinson recorded that the highest casualty number was twelve and that the bodies were brought back in carts and buried at an unknown place in the town. It is believed that wherever possible Civil War casualties were buried in churchyards and the enemy troops would likely have been left where they were killed or thrown into the River Trent if they were not taken away by their compatriots.

I would not rule out the possibility the skeletons represent evidence of a large execution site such as that excavated in the late 1960s at Walkington Wold in the East Ridings of Yorkshire where at some point between the late seventh and early eleventh centuries executions took place with the bodies dumped immediately beyond the boundary of the settlement.[388] The Walkington Wold burials were within a barrow. However, a natural feature such as a pond or tract of marshy land, if such a feature existed at Cranbrook Street, may have been considered to be appropriate. At Walkington Wold the absence of jaws from some of the skulls was interpreted as being evidence that the heads had been placed on stakes; a known Anglo-Saxon occurrence. At Cranbrook House, there were a number of skulls illustrated on Wass' plan, isolated from other remains, some of which have jaws missing, although how accurate Wass' plan was in this respect is unknown. Unfortunately there were no photographs of the stray skulls amongst his archive.

Wass failed to mention any trauma, if he would even have noticed or recognised any. Wass did not give any description of the state of the bones themselves and, of course, only fully excavated and studied one skeleton. The one surviving skeleton, skeleton V, is potentially missing its skull and even if the skull, which does not exhibit signs of trauma, does belong to skeleton V this does not preclude the possibility that the individual was executed by other means such as hanging, which is believed to have been the case of some of the individuals whose remains were excavated at Walkington Wold.

One photograph shows the presence of what looks like a coffin handle in a square shape cut, which may be showing the end of a coffin. If this object was associated with the skeletons then it would imply a post medieval date, though still predating 1820. However, I believe the object may be a cremation urn rather than a coffin and that it could have been buried at any time since cremation became legal in the twentieth century. It is not impossible it got buried in a back garden and its presence is entirely coincidental. It seems too strange that there were a large number of hurriedly buried humans with no coffins and then only one carefully buried coffin if all the burials are connected. For his own part, Wass only referred to the object as a handle on a small slip of paper with his negatives. Although the photograph of the object was on the same film as the Cranbrook House photographs it was not necessarily on the same site. It is interesting that Wass did not mention it at all in his paperwork for the Cranbrook House excavation.

If the object was at Cranbrook House the evidence regarding this object is not entirely conclusive, although it could be considered too much of a coincidence that what may possibly have been a coffin or casket was found on the same site as the disarticulated remains of a large number of individuals.

The fact is we simply cannot know how old the burials are except to say they predate 1820 and quite possibly the 1740s and 1677. Some of the human remains still survive, including partial fragments of three of the skulls. If funding was made available they could be subjected to carbon dating but obtaining funding is a very difficult task and so for the time being the mystery will continue. Yet despite the problems in Wass' recording of his discoveries, and the obvious difficulties in dating the burials, we should be grateful that Wass' excavation was undertaken at all, otherwise we would have had no knowledge about this previously unrecorded important site in the heart of the historic core.

The Secrets Which May Still Lie Beneath Our Feet: A View from 2014

The archaeological work and antiquarian observations have answered many questions but created many more puzzles which need to be solved by further archaeological work and study.

There has been a lack of archaeological work undertaken in the historic core of Nottingham over the past few years. With the economic downturn having reduced the amount of development across Britain, it has been inevitable that the amount of archaeology undertaken has massively reduced. Indeed since 2008 in the historic core there has only been a minor excavation at Nottingham Castle where a small section of the medieval castle's curtain wall was investigated after it was exposed by contractors making a toilet block, and further work by the Nottingham Historical and Archaeological Society who have been clearing out caves at the Broadmarsh Shopping Centre on Wednesday evenings. Excavations have been undertaken outside the historic core, such as at Lenton and Clifton in advance of the extension of the tramline, and at Wilford where I excavated the scant remains of a Late Iron Age settlement.

As a consequence of the limited amount of work having been carried out, very little has been contributed to our knowledge of Nottingham's past. Work has centred on research rather than excavations, with the Urban Archaeological Database and the Nottingham Caves Survey Project being the main projects, and the immediate future for field archaeology is bleak.

The Government's failure to introduce the Heritage White Paper and make it law is quite understandable at first sight. It was supposed to be announced during the Queen's opening of parliament in 2008 but tackling the recession was the obvious priority of the government. Now the role of archaeology in the planning process is less clear and has been weakened. Cuts to local government have compounded the problems. It can only be hoped that the already massive cuts of the past two decades do not threaten any further the already massively reduced archaeology team at the City Council which now consists of only one professional archaeologist.

Cuts to university funding and the lack of commercial archaeology opportunities are threatening the survival of archaeological field units. There is little or no income but staff require payment after all and so a large number of redundancies have taken place and archaeologists have, where they can, changed career.

Development might not be taking place which is resulting in a lack of archaeological work in the city centre but there is still plenty of discover and it could be discovered when development takes place as the economy will inevitably pick up. Yet when it does pick up who will be there to record it and ensure it is fully investigated? There will be fewer qualified and experienced archaeologists. There will still be a need, and obligation under the National Planning Policy Framework and the city's Local Development Framework, to record and remember rather than ignore and forget.

Despite major development in modern and historic times which destroyed and damaged archaeology, such as Maid Marian Way, Broadmarsh, the Great Central Railway cutting in the late nineteenth century and buildings with cellars and basements, there is still the potential for pockets of survival.

There is still much to uncover which would contribute tremendously to our knowledge of the development of the city, if and when some of the evidence is slowly uncovered provided the work is undertaken and recorded in a professional manner following archaeological guidelines.

There is a small area of the Halifax Place site which has not been developed upon and, if an excavation opportunity arises, could provide a wealth of information to help date the pottery kiln and find further evidence of timber buildings.

There is potential for work in caves old (those previously known about being opened up and investigated) and new (caves discovered occasionally even in the heart of the historic core of the medieval town during development). The Trent & Peak Archaeology project will continue to scan caves and we can only hope further funding will allow more caves to be scanned and interpreted.

Although the extant Broadmarsh Shopping Centre destroyed a great deal including part of a cave system, a stretch of the pre-Conquest ditch, evidence of early-medieval settlement not to mention features of historic interest such as Drury Hill itself, the plan to expand the centre will potentially enable archaeological investigation of important parts of the city. The River Leen, culverted beneath Canal Street and Castle Boulevard, organic, waterlogged deposits and evidence of tanning may all be encountered depending upon the finalised plans and provided that the planning application is approved.

Although the excavations for the extension of the tramway will be of limited depth there is the slight possibility that the stretches down towards West Bridgford may reveal something of archaeological interest. At the time of writing a large enclosure has been found during work in advance of the tramline extension, at Clifton, and on a nearby site where works for the A453 are taking place.

The plans to create a unique tourist attraction at Nottingham castle, if funding is made available, could see some important archaeological work undertaken which would both contribute to our knowledge of the site but also be an opportunity to make archaeology more accessible to the public.

Thus some questions may be answered and new ones may arise. Will we ever be able to answer any of the main questions? Will we ever know where the earliest caves were hewn? Will we ever have a better understanding of Iron Age Nottingham? Will we ever know if there was a Middle Saxon enclosed settlement or any occupation in the early Saxon period? Will we ever know what the significance was of Halifax Place during the Saxon period? And what about Whiston?

Will we ever find the town defences of the Civil War? Will we ever know what period the Cranbrook House burials date to? We can only speculate and opportunities to investigate may be few and far between and be on such a small scale that they prove inconclusive or are of little assistance if anything is found at all. Yet we must maintain hope that archaeological work, and research work on previous excavations, may yet yield even more knowledge of Nottingham's past.

Bibliography

Allen, D.F. 1961, 'Three Celtic Coins in Nottingham Castle Museum', *Transactions of the Thoroton Society of Nottinghamshire,* **65**, 7–9.

Anon. 1769, *A Description of England and Wales,* London: Newbery and Carnan.

Anon. 1904, 'The Precincts of Nottingham Castle,', *Transactions of the Thoroton Society of Nottinghamshire,* **8**, 38–41.

Anon. 1976, 'Untitled', *Transactions of the Thoroton Society of Nottinghamshire,* **80**, 81.

Anon. 1994, *Nottingham Castle Museum Lift Shaft Archaeological Report,* York Archaeological Trust.

Anon. 2003, *Archaeological Investigations in conjunction with Redevelopment of AC Gill, Fletcher Gate, Nottingham,* John Samuels Archaeological Consultants.

Baker, W.T. (ed.) 1900, *Records of the Borough of Nottingham, Volume V, 1625–1702,* Nottingham: Thomas Forman & Sons.

Bankes, R. 1609, *A Survey of Sherwood Forest.* Held by Nottinghamshire Archive.

Barley, M.W. 1959a, 'Notes: Nottinghamshire', *Medieval archaeology: journal of the Society for Medieval Archaeology,* **3**, 1959, 290–292.

Barley, M.W. 1959b, *East Midlands Archaeological Bulletin, 1959,* Nottingham: The University of Nottingham.

Barley, M.W. 1960, *East Midlands Archaeological Bulletin, 1960,* Nottingham: The University of Nottingham.

Barley, M.W. 1961, *East Midlands Archaeological Bulletin, 1961,* Nottingham: The University of Nottingham.

Barley, M.W. 1965, 'Nottingham Town Wall: Park Row Excavations 1964', *Transactions of the Thoroton Society of Nottinghamshire,* **69**, 50–65.

Barley, M.W. and Straw, I.F. 1969, 'Nottingham', *Historic Towns of the British Isles: Maps and Plans of Towns and Cities in the British Isles, with Historical Commentaries, from Earliest Times to 1800, Volume One,* Oxford: Oxford University Press.

Beckett, J (ed.) 2006, *A Centenary History of Nottingham,* Chichester: Phillimore & Co. Ltd.

Beeley, B.M. 1974, *East Midlands Archaeological Bulletin, 1974,* Nottingham: The University of Nottingham.

169

Beeley, B.M. 1977, *East Midlands Archaeological Bulletin, 1977,* Nottingham: The University of Nottingham.

Blackner, J. 1815, *The History of Nottingham,* Nottingham: Sutton and Son.

Bramley, J. 1938, 'St Peter's Church, Nottingham', *Transactions of the Thoroton Society of Nottinghamshire,* **42***,* 28–62.

Brand, K. 1984, 'The Park Estate, Nottingham: The Development of a Nineteenth Century Fashionable Suburb', *Transactions of the Thoroton Society of Nottinghamshire,* **88***,* 63–71.

Briscoe, J.P. 1908, *Chapters of Nottinghamshire History,* Nottingham: Derry & Sons.

Brown, C. 1896, *A History of Nottinghamshire,* London: E. Stock.

Brown, J. 2006, *Archaeological trial trench evaluation at The Broadmarsh, Nottingham,* Northamptonshire Archaeology, 5–6.

Buckberry, J.L. and Hadley, D.M. 2007, 'An Anglo Saxon Execution Cemetery at Walkington Wold, Yorkshire', *Oxford Journal of Archaeology,* **26(3)**, 309–329.

Burrows, B. and Cuttlerand, R. 2007, *Archaeological Excavation at St Mary's Gate/Warser Gate, Nottingham, Post-Excavation Assessment 2005–2006,* Birmingham Archaeology.

Burton, F.E. 1927, 'The Coins of King Athelstan of the Nottingham Mint', *Transactions of the Thoroton Society of Nottinghamshire,* **31***,* 106–107.

Burton, F.E. 1933, 'The Coins of King Canute of the Nottingham Mint', *Transactions of the Thoroton Society of Nottinghamshire,* **37***,* 41–44.

Butler, R.M. 1949, 'The Civil War defences of Nottingham', *Transactions of the Thoroton Society of Nottinghamshire,* **53***,* 26–33.

Campion, G.F. (ed.) 1938, *The Thoroton Society Excavation Section Annual Report for 1937*, Nottingham: The Thoroton Press.

Campion, G.F. (ed.) 1939, *The Thoroton Society Excavation Section Annual Report for 1938,* Nottingham: The Thoroton Press.

Campion, G.F. (ed.) 1940, *The Thoroton Society Excavation Section Annual Report for 1939,* Nottingham: The Thoroton Press.

Carter, A. 1971, 'Nottingham Town Wall: Park Row Excavation 1968', *Transactions of the Thoroton Society of Nottinghamshire,* **75***,* 33–40.

Charles, F.W.B. 1970, 'Severns', *Transactions of the Thoroton Society of Nottinghamshire,* **74***,* 45–61.

Clements, F. 1891, *Whence Nottingham Sprang,* Nottingham: F. Clements.

Corner, S. 1914, 'Education in the Middle Ages', *Transactions of the Thoroton Society of Nottinghamshire,* **18**, 66–82.

Crooke, D. 1984, 'Moothallgate and the Venue of the Nottinghamshire County Court in the Thirteenth Century', *Transactions of the Thoroton Society of Nottinghamshire,* **88**, 99–102.

BIBLIOGRAPHY

Cummins, W.A. and Moore, C.N. 1973, 'Petrological identification of
  stone implements from Lincolnshire, Nottinghamshire and Rutland',
  Proceedings of the Prehistoric Society, 39, 219–255.
Dawe, A. 1967, 'The pre conquest ditch near Bridlesmith Gate',
  Transactions of the Thoroton Society of Nottinghamshire, 71, 32–35.
Deering, C. 1751, *Nottingham Vetus et Nova*, Nottingham: George
  Ayscough & Thomas Wellington.
Defoe, D. 1734, *Curious and Diverting Journeys Thro' the Whole Island of
  Great Britain*, London: G. Parker.
Department for the Communities and Local Government. 2012,
  'Conserving and enhancing the historic environment', *National Planning
  Policy Framework*, <
  https://www.gov.uk/government/uploads/system/uploads/
  attachment_data/file/6077/2116950.pdf> [last accessed 30/03/2013].
Department of the Environment. 1972, *List of Buildings of Special
  Architectural or Historic Interest: City of Nottingham,* London:
  Department for the Environment.
Dobson, F.W. 1909, 'Nottingham Castle: Recent Explorations and some
  historical notes', *Transactions of the Thoroton Society of
  Nottinghamshire, 13, 143–159.*
Dobson, F.W. 1912, 'A Guard-room of the town wall of Nottingham',
  Transactions of the Thoroton Society of Nottinghamshire, 16, 159–163.
Drage, C. 1999, *Nottingham Castle: A Place Full Royal,* Nottingham:
  Nottingham Civic Society and The Thoroton Society of
  Nottinghamshire.
Evans, R. 1915, 'St Peter's Church, Nottingham', *Transactions of the
  Thoroton Society of Nottinghamshire, 19, 13–24.*
Farwell, D.E., Heaton, M. and Mepham, L. 1993, *5 George Street,
  Nottingham: Archaeological evaluation,* Wessex Archaeology.
F.H.T. 1961, *Brief History of "Sun" New Branch Premises: 24 and 26 Low
  Pavement*, Unpublished, held by Nottingham City Museums and
  Galleries.
Field, H. 1880, *The Date-Book of Remarkable Events Connected With
  Nottingham and its Neighbourhood, 1750–1879, from Authentic Records.*
  Nottingham: H. Field.
Gilbert, D. 2001, *Condition Survey of a portion of the medieval wall under
  Chapel Bar House, 1-5 Maid Marian Way, Nottingham,* Trent & Peak
  Archaeological Unit.
Gill, H. 1922, 'Notes on the Carmelite Friary at Nottingham', *Transactions
  of the Thoroton Society of Nottinghamshire, 26, 111–113.*
Gnanaratnam, T. 2000, *Archaeological watching brief at 21–23*

Bridlesmith Gate, Nottingham, University of Leicester Archaeological Services.

Gower, J.E.B., Mawer, A. and Stenton, F.M. 1940, *The Place Names of Nottinghamshire.*

Granger, J. 1904, *Old Nottingham: Its Streets, People, &c.: Second Series,* Nottingham: Nottingham Daily Press.

Granger, J. 1908, 'The Old Streets of Nottingham', *Transactions of the Thoroton Society of Nottinghamshire,* **12**, 95–124.

Gray, D. 1937, *The Thoroton Society Excavation Section Annual Report for 1936.* Nottingham: The Thoroton Press.

Haslam, J. 1987, 'The Second Burh of Nottingham', *Landscape History,* **9**, 45–52.

Heazell, E.H. 1925, 'Old Town Wall, Nottingham', *Transactions of the Thoroton Society of Nottinghamshire, Volume* **29**, 179–180.

Hine, T.C. 1876, *Nottingham, Its castle, a military fortress, a royal palace, a ducal mansion, a blackened ruin, a museum and gallery of art: with notes relating to the borough of Nottingham,* Nottingham: Hamilton, Adams, & Co.

Houldsworth, H. O. (ed.) 1949, *The Nottingham Archaeology Society Annual Report for 1948,* Nottingham: George Lomas Ltd.

Howard, R. 2009, 'A new Nottingham archaeological and mapping database', *The Nottinghamshire Historian,* **83**, 5–8.

Hunt, P.E. 1985, 'Excavations at the old High Pavement School, Nottingham', *Transactions of the Thoroton Society of Nottinghamshire,* **89**, 143–144.

Hutchinson, L. 1822, *Memoirs of the Life of Colonel Hutchinson,* London: Longman, Hurst, Rees, Orme, and Brown.

Ingram, J. 1823, *The Saxon Chronicle With an English Translation,* London: Longman, Hurst, Rees, Orme, and Brown.

Johnson, S. 2004, *Woolpack Lane, Nottingham: Interim Archaeological Summary,* John Samuels Archaeological Consultants.

Kinsley, G. 1994, *Excavations and Recording Work on Parts of Medieval and Post Medieval Buildings at Nottingham Shire Hall: Interim Summary Report,* Trent & Peak Archaeology.

Kinsley, G. 1996, *An Archaeological Watching Brief at Bath Street, Sneinton, Nottingham,* Trent & Peak Archaeology.

Kinsley, G. 1997a, *A Second Archaeological Watching Brief at Arnold and Carlton College, Bath Street, Sneinton, Nottingham, 1996,* Trent & Peak Archaeology.

Kinsley, G. 1997b, *An Archaeological Watching Brief at Island Street, Nottingham* Trent & Peak Archaeology.

Kinsley, G. 1999, *Nottingham Castle: An Archaeological Assessment,* Trent & Peak Archaeology.

Kinsley, G. 2000, *An Archaeological Excavation and Watching Brief on Repaving at Nottingham Castle,* Trent & Peak Archaeology.

Kinsley, G. 2003, *Surveys and Assessments of Caves and Underground Passages at Nottingham Castle,* Trent & Peak Archaeology.

Kinsley, G. 2004, *Nottingham Castle: Excavations Related to Service Installations 1998–9 Report and Archive*, Trent & Peak Archaeology.

Kinsley, G. 2005, *An Archaeological Survey and Evaluation of a Proposed Development Site at Garner's Hill, Nottingham,* Trent & Peak Archaeology.

Kinsley, G. 2006a, *Nottingham Castle Upper Bailey: An Archaeological Excavation and Watching Brief, April to September 2005,* Trent & Peak Archaeology.

Kinsley, G. 2006b, *An Archaeological Watching Brief at The Old Market Square, Nottingham,* Trent & Peak Archaeology.

Kinsley, G. 2006c, *Centre for Contemporary Arts, Garner's Hill, Nottingham: Interim Report on Pre-Construction Excavation*, Trent & Peak Archaeology.

Kinsley, G. 2006d, *An Archaeological Evaluation at the Newton Building, Nottingham Trent University*, Trent & Peak Archaeology.

Kinsley, G. and Brown, J. 1997, *An Archaeological Desk-Top Assessment of a Proposed Development Site at 26–28 Bridlesmith Gate, Nottingham,* Trent & Peak Archaeological Trust.

Kinsley, G., and Walker, D. 1999, *Walls Exposed After a Rock Fall at Nottingham Castle, Deceber 1996 Report and Archive,* Trent & Peak Archaeology.

Knight, D., Lomax, S., Young, G. 2013, 'The Origins of Nottingham: Archaeological Investigations in the Medieval Town From 1969 to 1980', *Transactions of the Thoroton Society of Nottinghamshire,* **116**, 45–52 .

Laird, F.C. 1813, *A historical and topographical description of the county of Nottingham,* London: Sherwood, Neely and Jones.

Laxton, R.R., Litton, C.D. and Howard, R.E. 1995, 'Nottinghamshire houses dated by Dendrochronology', *Transactions of the Thoroton Society of Nottinghamshire,* **99**, 45–54.

Lomax, S. 2011, 'Cranbrook House, Cranbrook Street, Nottingham: An Archaeological Excavation Revisited', *Transactions of the Thoroton Society of Nottinghamshire,* **115**, 17–30.

Lucas, J. 1994, *Nottingham General Hospital: Specification SJL94/223 for full excavation of Zone 2A,* University of Leicester Archaeological Services.

MacCormick, A.G. 2001, 'Nottingham's Underground Maltings and Other Medieval Caves: Architecture and Dating', *Transactions of the Thoroton Society of Nottinghamshire,* **105**, 73–100.

MacCormick, A.G. and Waltham, T. 1993, 'The caves, malt kiln and tannery at the Black's Head site, Nottingham', *Transactions of the Thoroton Society of Nottinghamshire,* **97**, 64–73.

Malone, S. 2001, *Archaeological Watching Brief on Land at 14 Plumptre Street, Nottingham,* Archaeological Project Services.

Marsden, J.F., 2001, *An Archaeological Evaluation and Exhumation at Nottingham Ice Stadium, Lower Parliament Street, Nottingham, Interim Report,* John Samuels Archaeological Consultants.

Mastoris, S.N. 1981, 'The boundary between the English and French boroughs of medieval Nottingham: A documentary survey', *Transactions of the Thoroton Society of Nottinghamshire,* **85**, 68–75.

May, J. 1962, *East Midlands Archaeological Bulletin, 1962,* Nottingham: The University of Nottingham.

May, J. 1963, *East Midlands Archaeological Bulletin, 1963,* Nottingham: The University of Nottingham.

May, J. 1964, *East Midlands Archaeological Bulletin, 1964,* Nottingham: The University of Nottingham.

May, J. 1965, *East Midlands Archaeological Bulletin, 1965,* Nottingham: The University of Nottingham.

May, J. 1966, *East Midlands Archaeological Bulletin, 1966,* Nottingham: The University of Nottingham.

Metcalf, D.M. 1998, *An Atlas of Anglo Saxon and Norman Coin Finds,* Oxford: Ashmolean Museum.

Orange, J. 1840, *A History and Antiquities of Nottingham (Volume I),* London: Hamilton, Adams and Co.

Owen, J.F. and Walsby, J.C. 1989, *A Register of Nottingham's Caves,* Nottingham: British Geological Survey.

Page, W. (ed.) 1906, *Victoria History of the Counties of England: Nottinghamshire Volume I,* London: Archibald Constable and Company.

Page, W. (ed.). 1910, *Victoria History of the Counties of England: Nottinghamshire Volume II,* London: Archibald Constable and Company.

Parker, A. 1932, 'Nottingham Pottery', *Transactions of the Thoroton Society of Nottinghamshire,* **36**, 79–134.

Parker, A. 1935, 'Exhibition of Relics of Old Nottingham and District', *Transactions of the Thoroton Society of Nottinghamshire,* **39**, 119–125.

Ponsford, M.W. 1971, 'Nottingham Town Wall: Park Row Excavation 1967', *Transactions of the Thoroton Society of Nottinghamshire,* **75**, 5–32.

Potter, H.R. 1962, *Report on the History of the River Leen Near Nottingham,* Nottingham: Trent River Board.

Roberts, J.S. 1868, *The Legendary Ballads of England and Scotland,* London: Frederick Warne and Co.

Roffe, D. Undated, *Nottinghamshire and the North,* <http://roffe.co.uk/phd/phd100.htm> [accessed 26 March 2013].

Roffe, D. 2000, *Pre-conquest Nottingham,* <http://www.roffe.co.uk/nottingham.htm> [accessed 26 March 2013].

Shipman, J. 1899a, *Notes on The Old Town Wall of Nottingham Being A Description of some Recent Exposures of it,* Nottingham: Frank Murray.

Shipman, J. 1899b, *Excavations at the Nottingham General Hospital, the New Wing, Interesting Discoveries With a Plan,* Nottingham: Frank Murray.

Smith, F and Taylor, E. 1941, *The Thoroton Society Excavation Section Annual Report for 1940,* Nottingham: The Thoroton Press.

Smith, F and Taylor, E. 1942, *The Nottingham Archaeology Society Annual Report for 1941,* Nottingham: The Thoroton Press.

Speede, J. 1610, 'The Countie of Nottingham described The Shire Townes Situation and the Earls thereof observed', *The Theatre of the Empire of Great Britain,* London: John Sudbury and George Humble.

Stapleton, A. 1904, *An Historical Sketch of the Caves of Old Nottingham and The Nottinghamshire Coalfield: some notes regarding its ancient history* <http://www.nottshistory.org.uk/monographs/caves1904/caves1.htm> [accessed 05/04/2013].

Stapleton, A. 1912, 'Nottingham Town Wall', *Transactions of the Thoroton Society of Nottinghamshire,* **16**, 135–149.

Stevenson, W.H. (ed.) 1882, *Records of the Borough of Nottingham, Volume I, 1155–1399,* Nottingham: Thomas Forman & Sons.

Stevenson, W.H. (ed.) 1883, *Records of the Borough of Nottingham, Volume II, 1399–1485,* Nottingham: Thomas Forman & Sons.

Stevenson, W.H. (ed.) 1885, *Records of the Borough of Nottingham, Volume III, 1485–1547,* Nottingham: Thomas Forman & Sons.

Stevenson, W.H. (ed.) 1889, *Records of the Borough of Nottingham, Volume IV, 1547–1625,* Nottingham: Thomas Forman & Sons.

Stevenson, W.H. 1912, 'The great ditch, St Mary's Hill, Nottingham', *Transactions of the Thoroton Society of Nottinghamshire,* **16**, 151–154.

Stevenson, W. 1918, *Transactions of the Thoroton Society of Nottinghamshire,* **22**, 51–74.

Stevenson, W. and Stapleton, A. 1895, *The Religious Institutions of Old Nottingham, Volume I,* Nottingham: T. Forman and Sons.

Stevenson, W. and Stapleton, A. 1898, *The Religious Institutions of Old Nottingham, Volume II,* Nottingham: T. Forman and Sons.

Stevenson, W.H., (ed.) 1904, *Asser's Life of King Alfred,* Oxford: Oxford University Press.

Stretton, W. 1910, *The Stretton Manuscripts: BEING NOTES ON THE HISTORY OF NOTTINGHAMSHIRE,* Nottingham: Privately published.

Stukeley, W. 1724, *Itinerarium Curiosum, Or, an Account of the Antiquitys and Remarkable Curiositys in Nature Or Art, Observ'd in Travels Thro' Great Britain, Centuria 1,* London: W. Stukeley.

Sutton, J.S. 1852, *The Date-book of Remarkable and Memorable Events Connected with Nottingham and Its Neighbourhood: 1750–1850,* London: Simpkin & Marshall.

Thoroton, R. 1797, *History of Nottinghamshire,* London: J. Throsby.

Wadsworth, F. A. 1918, 'The Parish Churches and houses of Friars of Nottingham, their Chapels, Gilds, Images and Lights', *Transactions of the Thoroton Society of Nottinghamshire,* **22**, 75–111.

Walker, D. 2006, *An Archaeological Watching Brief at Western Street, Nottingham,* Trent & Peak Archaeology.

Walker, J.H. 1928, 'An Itinerary of Nottingham', *Transactions of the Thoroton Society of Nottinghamshire,* **32**, 30–36.

Walker, J.H. 1929, 'An Itinerary of Nottingham', *Transactions of the Thoroton Society of Nottinghamshire,* **33**, 23–71.

Walker, J.H. 1931, 'An Itinerary of Nottingham', *Transactions of the Thoroton Society of Nottinghamshire,* **35**, 70–91.

Walker, J.H. 1932, 'An Itinerary of Nottingham', *Transactions of the Thoroton Society of Nottinghamshire,* **36**, 1–27.

Walker, J.H. 1933, 'An Itinerary of Nottingham', *Transactions of the Thoroton Society of Nottinghamshire,* **37**, 1–10 .

Walker, J.H. 1943, *Schedule of Objects of antiquarian interest in Nottingham which are worthy of preservation,* Unpublished, held by Nottingham City Museums and Galleries.

Walker, V.W. (ed.). 1945, *The Nottingham Archaeology Society Annual Report for 1944,* Nottingham: The Thoroton Press.

Walker, V.W. (ed.), 1946, *The Nottingham Archaeology Society Annual Report for 1945,* Nottingham: The Thoroton Press.

Walker, V.W. (ed.). 1947, *The Nottingham Archaeology Society Annual Report for 1946,* Nottingham: The Thoroton Press.

Walker, V.W. (ed.), 1948, *The Nottingham Archaeology Society Annual Report for 1947,* Nottingham: George Lomas Ltd.

Waltham, T. 1992, *The Sandstone Caves of Nottingham*, Nottingham: East Midlands Geological Society.

Waltham, T. 1994, 'The Sandstone Mines of Nottingham', *Bulletin of the Peak District Mines Historical Society,* **12(4)**, 1–11.

Wass, D. A. 1961a, *Curry's, Carlton Street* (part of the unpublished Tony Wass archive held by Nottingham City Museums and Galleries).

Wass, D. A. 1961b, *The Black Swan* (part of the unpublished Tony Wass archive held by Nottingham City Museums and Galleries).

Wheeler, H. 1978, *East Midlands Archaeological Bulletin, 1978,* Nottingham: The University of Nottingham.

Wheeler, H. and Fowkes, D. 1982, *East Midlands Archaeological Bulletin, 1979–1982,* Nottingham: The University of Nottingham.

White, W. 1832, *History, gazetteer, and directory of Nottinghamshire, and the town and county of the town of Nottingham*, Sheffield: Sheffield Independent.

Wildgoose, R.H. 1961, 'The defences of the pre-conquest borough of Nottingham', *Transactions of the Thoroton Society of Nottinghamshire,* **65***,* 19–26.

Wilson, D.M. and Hurst, D.G. 1966, 'Medieval Britain in 1965', *Medieval archaeology: journal of the Society for Medieval Archaeology,* **10***,* 168–219.

Wylie, W.H. 1853, [389]*Old and New Nottingham,* London: Longman, Hurst, Rees, Orme, and Brown.

Young, C.S.B, 1975, 'An excavation in Brewhouse Yard, Nottingham', *Transactions of the Thoroton Society of Nottinghamshire,* **79***,* 14–15.

Young, C.S.B. 1983, *Discovering Rescue Archaeology in Nottingham,* Nottingham: Nottingham City Museums.

Young, C.S.B. 1986, 'Archaeology in Nottingham: the pre-Conquest Borough', *History in the Making: Recent Historical Research In Nottingham and Nottinghamshire, 1985,* 1–4.

Young, G.A.B. 1987, 'Archaeology in Nottingham: the Halifax Place excavation', *History in the Making: Recent Historical Research In Nottingham and Nottinghamshire, 1986,* 1–6.

Youngs, S.M. and Clark, J. 1982, 'Medieval Britain in 1981', *Medieval archaeology: journal of the Society for Medieval Archaeology,* **26***,* 202–203.

Notes

[1] Roffe 2000
[2] Page 1906, 203–204
[3] Laird 1813, 78
[4] Howard 2009, 5–6
[5] Knight, Lomax and Young 2013, 45–52
[6] http://www.archaeologydataservice.ac.uk
[7] Mastoris 1981, 68–75
[8] Roffe Undated
[9] Mastoris 1981, 68–75
[10] Barley and Straw 1969, 5
[11] Department for the Communities and Local Government 2012
[12] Waltham 1992, 1–2
[13] Wildgoose 1961, 19–26
[14] Nottinghamshire Historic Environment Record, reference 00493
[15] Cummins and Moore 1973, 219–255
[16] Beeley 1977, 46
[17] *Nottinghamshire Gazetteer Committee Index*
[18] English Heritage, *National Monuments Record,* NMR_NATINV-317871
[19] Page 1906, 188–189
[20] *Nottinghamshire Gazetteer Committee Index*
[21] Young 1983
[22] Lucas 1994
[23] Young 1983
[24] Ingram 1823, 52
[25] Roffe Undated
[26] Roffe Undated
[27] Young 1986, 1–4
[28] Haslam 1987, 45–52
[29] Burton 1927, 106–107
[30] Roffe 2000
[31] Roffe 2000
[32] Drage 1999, 14
[33] Roffe 2000
[34] Drage 1999, 14, 37–39
[35] Corner 1914, 77
[36] Barley and Straw 1969, 3
[37] Crooke 1984, 100
[38] Halifax Place archive (unpublished)
[39] Shipman 1899a, 69–70
[40] Barley and Straw 1969, 4

NOTES

[41] Deering, 1751, 16
[42] Stevenson and Stapleton 1898
[43] Drage 1999, 68
[44] Speede 1610
[45] Hutchinson 1822, 114
[46] Hutchinson, 1822
[47] Hutchinson 1822, 357–358
[48] Defoe1734 , 330; Drage 1999, 19
[49] Drage 1999, 19
[50] Mastoris 1981, 68–75
[51] Defoe 1734, 329–333
[52] Hutchinson 1822
[53] Clements 1891
[54] Campion 1938, 26
[55] Allen 1961, 8–9
[56] Stevenson 1912, 151–154
[57] Young, 1983
[58] Young, 1983
[59] Department for Communities and Local Government 2012
[60] The Campion Archive
[61] Gray 1937, 28–30
[62] Potter 1962
[63] Excavation Archive for Brewhouse Yard (WW75); Young 1975, 14–15
[64] Kinsley 1997b
[65] Stevenson 1918, 73
[66] *The Nottingham Journal*, 3 March 1880
[67] The Thoroton Society of Nottinghamshire Archaeological Section News Letter, 3 Feb 1969
[68] Orange 1840, 14
[69] Stevenson 1882, 179
[70] Stevenson 1885, 255
[71] Wylie 1853, 277–278
[72] Hutchinson 1822, 276
[73] White 1832, 189–190
[74] Brown 2006
[75] Haslam 1987, 45–52
[76] Stevenson and Stapleton 1898, 120–130
[77] Stevenson and Stapleton 1898, 75–87
[78] Blackner 1815, 18
[79] Walker 1943, 34
[80] Barley and Straw 1969, 1
[81] Campion 1938, 24
[82] Huntingdon Street Kitchens excavation archive (unpublished)
[83] Young 1983
[84] Gower, Mawer and Stenton 1940, 20
[85] Deering 1751, 73
[86] Shipman 1899a

[87] Shipman, 1899a, 14
[88] The Campion Archive (unpublished)
[89] The Campion Archive (unpublished)
[90] Campion 1938, 23–25
[91] Tony Wass archive (unpublished)
[92] Barley 1959b, 14
[93] Page 1906, 47
[94] Page 1906, 222
[95] Nottinghamshire Historic Environment Record, reference 00493
[96] Beeley 1977, 46
[97] English Heritage, *National Monuments Record,* NMR_NATINV-317585
[98] Cummins and Moore 1973, 219–255
[99] English Heritage, *National Monuments Record,* NMR_NATINV-317881
[100] *Nottinghamshire Gazetteer Committee Index*
[101] English Heritage, *National Monuments Record,* NMR_NATINV-317871
[102] Page 1906, 188–9
[103] *The Nottinghamshire Gazetteer Committee Index*
[104] Fisher Gate archive (unpublished)
[105] Young 1983
[106] Halifax Place archive (unpublished)
[107] Lucas 1994
[108] Kinsley 1999
[109] White 1864, 72–73
[110] Young 1983
[111] Young 1986, 1–4
[112] Marsden 2001
[113] Young 1983
[114] Halifax Place archive (unpublished)
[115] Ingram 1823, 52
[116] Young 1986, 1–4
[117] Roffe 2000
[118] Roffe 2000
[119] Page 1906, 203 - 204
[120] Page 1906, 203–204
[121] Roffe 2000
[122] Kinsley 1996; Kinsley 1997a
[123] Wildgoose 1961, 19–26
[124] Wildgoose 1961, 19–26
[125] Wildgoose 1961, 19–26
[126] Wass 1961a
[127] Wass 1961b; Wildgoose 1961, 19–26
[128] Wass 1961b; Wildgoose 1961, 19–26
[129] Dawe 1967, 32–35
[130] Drury Hill excavation archive (unpublished)
[131] Woolpack Lane excavation archive (unpublished)
[132] Gnanaratnam 2000
[133] Bankes 1609

NOTES

[134] Roffe 2000
[135] Young 1987, 1–6
[136] Halifax Place excavation archive (unpublished)
[137] Drury Hill archive (unpublished)
[138] Boots Garage archive (unpublished)
[139] Anon 2003
[140] Malone 2001
[141] Metcalf 1998, 166, 304
[142] Stevenson 1912, 151–153
[143] Burton 1927, 106–107
[144] Burton 1933, 41–44
[145] Thoroton 1797, Plan
[146] Brown 1896, Chapter 1
[147] Drage 1999, 98
[148] Anon 1904, 38–41
[149] Dobson 1909, 143–159
[150] Dobson 1909, 143–159
[151] Gray 1937, 11
[152] Drage 1999, 75-78, 81–94
[153] Drage 1999, 75-78, 81–94
[154] Drage 1999, 78
[155] Drage 1999, 78, 135
[156] Youngs and Clark 1982, 202–203
[157] Drage 1999, 95–98
[158] Drage (unpublished site notebook)
[159] Kinsley 1999
[160] Anon 1994
[161] Kinsley and Walker 1999
[162] Gordon Young, *pers. comm.*
[163] Kinsley 2004
[164] Kinsley 2004
[165] Kinsley 2004
[166] Kinsley 2000
[167] Kinsley 2000
[168] Kinsley 2000
[169] Kinsley 2006a
[170] Kinsley 2006a
[171] Kinsley 2006a.
[172] Walker 1948, 7–9
[173] English Heritage, *National Monuments Record,* NMR_NATINV-317521
[174] Drage 1999, 59
[175] Drage 1999, 59
[176] Hutchinson 1822, 165–167
[177] Barley 1965, 50–65
[178] Ponsford 1971, 5–32; Carter 1971, 33–40
[179] Wheeler 1978, 44
[180] Woolpack Lane archive (unpublished)

[181] Young 1983
[182] Young 1983
[183] Stapleton 1912, 146
[184] Shipman 1899a, 69–70
[185] Orange 1840, 79–80
[186] Deering 1751, 14
[187] Stapleton 1912, 135–149
[188] Stapleton 1912, 135–149
[189] Stapleton 1912, 135–149
[190] Stapleton 1912, 135–149
[191] Shipman1899a, 49–52
[192] Shipman 1899a, 43–49
[193] Stapleton 1912, 142
[194] Heazell 1925, 179–180
[195] Campion 1939, 30
[196] Barley 1959a, 290–292
[197] Barley 1965, 50–65
[198] Ponsford 1971, 5–32; Carter 1971, 33–40
[199] Wheeler 1978, 44
[200] Wheeler 1978, 44
[201] Gilbert 2001
[202] Stapleton 1912, 137 - 141
[203] Walker 1931, 70–71
[204] Shipman 1899a, 76–77
[205] Stapleton 1912, 141
[206] Stretton 1910, 163
[207] Stretton 1910, 164
[208] Stapleton 1912, 145
[209] Granger 1908, 119–120
[210] Orange 1840, 81
[211] Deering 1751, 14
[212] Barley and Straw 1969, 3
[213] Fisher Gate archive (unpublished)
[214] Dobson 1912, 159–163
[215] Dobson 1912, 159–163
[216] Deering 1751, 14
[217] Smith and Taylor 1942, 6
[218] Kinsley 2006b
[219] Mastoris 1981, 68–75
[220] Barley and Straw 1969, 5
[221] Mastoris 1981, 68–75
[222] Barley and Straw 1969, 2
[223] Barley and Straw 1969, 2
[224] Orange 1840, 88–89
[225] Stevenson 1882, 157; Bramley 1938, 28–62
[226] Drury Hill archive (unpublished)
[227] Kinsley 2006c

NOTES

228 Drury Hill archive (unpublished)
229 Halifax Place archive (unpublished)
230 Halifax Place archive (unpublished)
231 Fisher Gate archive (unpublished)
232 Goose Gate archive (unpublished)
233 Boots Garage archive (unpublished)
234 Barley and Straw 1969, 4
235 Barley and Straw 1969, 4
236 Deering 1751, 16
237 Charles 1970, 45–61
238 Charles 1970, 45–61
239 *Vernacular Architecture, Volume 15,* 68
240 Walker 1932, 15
241 Laxton, Litton and Howard 1995, 49
242 *Vernacular Architecture, Volume 27,* 87
243 Anon 1976, 81
244 Gnaratnam 2000
245 Kinsley and Brown 1997
246 Alan MacCormick *pers. comm.*
247 Speede 1610
248 Stevenson and Stapleton 1898, 157
249 Walker 1928, 30–36
250 Deering 1751, 19–20
251 Wylie 1853, 90–91
252 Owen and Walsby 1989, 6
253 Walker 1933, 5
254 Deering, 1751, 34
255 Evans, 1915, 13
256 Field, 1880, 624-625
257 Nottingham City Museums and Galleries, *Report to the Arts Director, Leisure Services [Archaeology] Sub Committee, 17 July 1989;* Nottingham City Museums and Galleries, *Report to the Arts Director, Leisure Services [Archaeology] Sub Committee, 14 October 1991*
258 Walker 1929, 49
259 Barley and Straw 1969, Map of the medieval and post medieval town of Nottingham
260 Hutchinson 1822, 276
261 Nottingham City Museums and Galleries, *Report to the Arts Director, Leisure Services [Archaeology] Sub Committee, 14 October 1991*
262 Stevenson and Stapleton 1895, 49
263 Gill 1922, 111–113
264 Field 1880, 55–56
265 Field 1880, 464
266 Stevenson and Stapleton 1895, 49
267 Stevenson and Stapleton 1895, 62
268 Walker 1948, 8
269 Wilson and Hurst 1966, 199
270 Crooke 1984, 99–102

[271] Stevenson and Stapleton 1895, 38–63

[272] The Campion Archive

[273] Campion 1938, 18

[274] Stevenson and Stapleton 1895, 74

[275] Campion 1938, 19–20

[276] Corner 1914, 77

[277] Speede 1610

[278] Wadsworth 1918, 79

[279] Wadsworth 1918, 79

[280] Stevenson and Stapleton 1895, 26–38

[281] Stevenson and Stapleton 1895, 26–38

[282] Stevenson and Stapleton 1898, 196

[283] Stevenson and Stapleton 1895, 26–38

[284] Stevenson and Stapleton 1898, 120–130

[285] *The Nottinghamshire Guardian*, 'Local Notes and Queries', 15 March 1919

[286] Stevenson and Stapleton 1898, 120–130

[287] Briscoe 1908, 3

[288] Sutton 1852, 401–402

[289] Orange 1840, 88–89

[290] Stevenson 1882, 430

[291] Sutton 1852, 473; Stevenson and Stapleton 1898, 140, 142

[292] Sutton 1852, 133–144

[293] Sutton 1852, 133–144

[294] Stevenson and Stapleton 1898, 133–144 , 159–161

[295] Stevenson and Stapleton 1898, 156

[296] *The Nottingham Journal* 14 September 1878; Stevenson and Stapleton 1898, 142–143

[297] Stevenson and Stapleton 1898, 143–144

[298] Stevenson and Stapleton 1898, 139; Roberts 1868, 612

[299] Stevenson 1904, 24

[300] Anon 1769, 137

[301] Campion 1938, 24–26

[302] MacCormick 2001, 73–100

[303] Campion 1938, 27–28

[304] Stapleton 1904, 17–20

[305] Johnson 2004

[306] Stapleton 1904, 26–27

[307] Owen and Walsby 1989, 1

[308] Stevenson 1889, 283

[309] Hine, 1876

[310] Hine, 1876

[311] F. H. T. 1961

[312] Deering 1751, 15

[313] MacCormick 2001, 73–100

[314] Nottingham City Museums and Galleries, *Report to the Arts Director, Leisure Services [Archaeology] Sub Committee, 23 April 1990*

[315] Beeley 1974, 45–46

[316] Deering 1751, 15

NOTES

317 Nottingham City Museums and Galleries, *Report to the Arts Director, Leisure Services [Archaeology] Sub Committee, 23 April 1990*

318 Owen and Walsby 1989, 2

319 Belley 1977, 57–58

320 Kinsley 2003, 6

321 Campion 1940, 6–8

322 Owen and Walsby 1989, 1–6

323 MacCormick and Waltham 1993, 64–73

324 The Campion Archive

325 Walker 1947, 9

326 MacCormick 2001, 73–100

327 Shipman 1899a, 23–43

328 Shipman 1899b

329 Owen and Walsby 1989, 1; Drage 1999, 50–51

330 Owen and Walsby 1989, 2

331 Waltham 1994

332 Waltham 1994

333 Waltham 1994

334 Waltham 1994

335 Waltham 1992, 15–16

336 Waltham 1992, 15–16

337 Owen and Walsby 1989, 2

338 Brand 1984, 63–71

339 *The Nottingham Guardian Journal*, 28 January 1928

340 Walker 1948, 5–6

341 Department of the Environment 1972

342 *Nottingham Evening Post,* 31 October 1989

343 Barley and Straw 1969, 3

344 Halifax Place excavation archive (unpublished).

345 Vicky Nailor *pers. comm.*

346 Goose Gate excavation archive (unpublished)

347 Campion 1938, 20–21

348 Walker 2006

349 Parker 1932, 123–124

350 Farwell, Heaton and Mepham 1993

351 Parker 1932, 83–84

352 Parker 1932, 83–84

353 Walker 1931, 85

354 Campion 1940, 12

355 Belley 1977, 58; *The Nottingham Guardian Journal*, 14 December 1970

356 Granger 1904, 42–43

357 Brown 2006

358 Boots Garage excavation archive (unpublished)

359 Halifax Place excavation archive (unpublished)

360 Hunt 1985, 143–144

361 Kinsley 1994

362 Kinsley 2005

[363] MacCormick 2001, 73–100

[364] Alan MacCormick *pers. comm.*

[365] Burrows and Cuttlerand 2007

[366] Fisher Gate excavation archive (unpublished)

[367] Hutchinson 1822, 233–235

[368] Hutchinson 1822 , 157

[369] Drage 1999, 78, 135

[370] Hutchinson 1822, 274–275

[371] Deering 1751, 62

[372] Baker 1900, 207–208

[373] Hutchinson, L., 1822, 222

[374] Deering 1751, 165–166

[375] Butler 1949, 26–33

[376] Hutchinson 1822, 236–237

[377] Hutchinson 1822, 268

[378] Butler 1949, 26–33

[379] Shipman 1899a, 17–19

[380] Kinsley 2006d

[381] Ponsford 1971, 5–32

[382] Fisher Gate archive (unpublished)

[383] Sutton 1852, 144

[384] Thoroton 1797, 31

[385] Hutchinson 1822, 286

[386] Lomax 2011, 17–30

[387] *The Nottingham Evening Post,* 18 July 1962

[388] Parker 1935, 122

[389] Buckberry and Hadley 2007, 309 – 329

Index

Historic references 110
Windmill, The 94
Woolpack Lane 29, 53, 54, 71,
 119
 Excavation in 1970 29, 53, 71

York Archaeological Trust 31,
 65
Young, Charles S. B. 28, 156
Young, Gordon A. B. 10, 119,
 160